IMAGES
of America

DOWNTOWN
STOCKTON

VIEW OF THE WEBER HOME FROM BANNER ISLAND, OCTOBER 1851. The Weber's home sat on Weber Point facing west toward the Stockton Channel. The gardens surrounding the home were an attraction in early Stockton. C.M. Weber regularly watched ships arrive from the cupola of the house.

IMAGES
of America

DOWNTOWN
STOCKTON

Daniel Kasser

ARCADIA
PUBLISHING

Published by Arcadia Publishing
Charleston, South Carolina

Library of Congress Catalog Card Number: 2004112270

For all general information contact Arcadia Publishing at:
Telephone 843-853-2070
Fax 843-853-0044
E-mail sales@arcadiapublishing.com
For customer service and orders:
Toll-Free 1-888-313-2665

Visit us on the Internet at www.arcadiapublishing.com

HEAD OF NAVIGATION, STOCKTON CHANNEL, 1872. The head of navigation has been the subject of countless photographs of Stockton since the city was first settled. It has become a barometer of Stockton's changing fortunes.

CONTENTS

ACKNOWLEDGMENTS

This publication is anchored in opportunities to work with wonderful people and collaborators over the last 10 years. My thanks to:

Tod Ruhstaller and the staff at the Haggin Museum in Stockton. They extended my first opportunity to survey the archives in 1992 and tell the story of Stockton photographers. Many of the photographs in this publication are here courtesy of the Haggin.

Helen Kennedy Cahill and Moira Kennedy Holden. They gave me the opportunity to work with the Rulofson Daguerreotypes of Stockton and the Weber-Murphy Archive when this odyssey began many years ago. Their support moved the Stockton Re-photographic Survey into the digital age.

The University of the Pacific's Holt-Atherton Special Collections Library: Shaun Sutton, current director, and Daryl Morrison, former director; Donald Walker, archivist (ret.); and especially Janene Ford, archive assistant (ret.), for her always lovely manner and knowledgeable navigation through the V. Covert Martin Collection; Annie Holden, archivist, for her assistance in gathering the materials for this publication on short notice.

Lucinda Kasser for her discerning editing skills and especially her support through all that this has required to assemble.

Lana Marenco and Chris Robb who scanned and touched up many of the photographs for this publication.

University of the Pacific, Committee for Scholarly and Artistic Activity Grants, without which this project would have been impossible in the short time allotted for its completion.

Horrace Spencer for his humor and perspective on the history of Stockton.

Leslie Crow for her early collaborations with the Stockton Re-photographic Survey.

My many students over the years, too numerous to list here, who have participated in the Stockton Re-photographic Survey.

Peter Palmquist, whose untimely passing prevents a personal expression of my gratitude for all he has done for the history of photography.

The photographs reproduced in this book were edited from the Archives of the University of the Pacific and the Haggin Museum. Many of the images are held by both institutions.

INTRODUCTION

Living in Stockton today, one cannot help but read and hear concerned discussion about downtown Stockton. What was and what is downtown Stockton? As a photographer and teacher in the community I have taken the time to research and think about these questions. I have found that downtown Stockton has many stories, with each generation of Stocktonians contributing a distinctive view. Stockton's first name was Tuleberg. In the years that followed, many names were given and popularized by travelers who visited here: the slough city, the windmill city, the tree city, the brick city, the gas city, all of which were accurate descriptions of a rapidly changing Stockton.

The momentum of the city's development provided cause and content for the work of Stockton's photographers. Their images reveal what was important to the city's inhabitants through its first century. Between 1850 and 1950, eight prominent photographers recorded the early settlement and spectacular rise of Stockton, from a rough, gold rush depot to a major Californian metropolis. Their extraordinary images document an odyssey of argonauts and pioneers; entrepreneurs, who, detouring from the gold trail, settled and built their fortunes here. Their achievements and world-changing innovations produced a golden era for Stockton.

Stockton became an incorporated city in 1850. Attempts at settlement began in 1843 when Stockton's founder, Charles M. Weber, acquired the Spanish land grant for Rancho Campo de los Franceses. Stabilized settlement began in 1847 at the head of navigation for the Stockton Channel, a tributary to the San Joaquin River. The lake north of the channel head (McLeod's Lake) was once an abundant beaver pond that attracted French trappers to the region earlier in the century. To the south of the lake, Charles and Helen Murphy-Weber maintained a modestly scaled, lavishly furnished home on what is today Weber Point. The Weber home was surrounded by spectacular gardens that inspired city planning and visitors to Stockton.

Weber's plan for Stockton aimed to create an efficient, modern, well-drained and -ventilated city. Stockton was planned and mapped two times between 1849 and 1851. The plan took shape upon a grid overlaying a natural system of small sloughs that flowed westward through the city. Weber's vision for a modern Stockton and community identity was achieved in relatively large increments. The construction of the first county courthouse in 1853–1854 provided a more certain identity for the community and a new era for Stockton. Abundance and adversity became Stockton's muses prompting drastic modifications to city planning. From 1855 to 1900, a procession of devastating fires and floods produced great loss and hardship in Stockton. These disasters prompted the truncation of natural waterways running through the city and motivated an eastward migration of Stockton's commercial district. Despite these challenges, Stockton optimized its strategic geographic location at the crossroads of California. Coordinating interstate water and rail transportation with interurban systems helped to make Stockton a popular destination for late 19th- and early 20th-century tourists seeking entertainment and recreation, creating the epitome of the sylvan California lifestyle.

Judging from the remarkable number of photographs made of Stockton's early civic and cultural institutions, Stocktonians were very proud of their city. Between 1850 and 1940 Stocktonians built an impressive directory of civic, cultural and commercial buildings. Many of these buildings remain in Stockton today.

Photographs also record Stockton's swift trajectory to become a world-class manufacturing city during its golden age. The city became the hub of an agricultural revolution that began between 1870 and 1900. This is the legacy of an extraordinary group of industrial artists, manufacturing entrepreneurs, and merchants who creatively tackled significant obstacles in agriculture and industry. Their industrial innovations and agricultural machines have been exported to international markets. These extraordinary people sparked a sizeable local economy, personal wealth, and a dynamic downtown Stockton. This legacy continues. San Joaquin County has remained among the top agricultural counties in the nation for nearly a century.

Stockton's golden era occurred between 1900 and 1945. By that time downtown had reinvented itself from rough and dusty gold rush depot, to bucolic village, to a commercial center by day and "bright lights, big city" by night. Stockton's pulse was taken from Main Street. Swanky residential hotels, public baths, nightclubs, and an assortment of tawdry venues balanced urban life. Stockton became a significant entertainment and recreation destination in California. Its centrally located hotels and transportation systems connected a menu of pleasure that once bolstered Stockton's reputation as a "show town" and recreational mecca. While downtown Stockton was first a product of the bountiful surrounding farmland, popular entertainment in theatres and nightclubs made the Stockton experience complete and memorable. But the good times did not last. The war years were hard on Stockton. The disasters of war did not end with peace and prosperity. In hindsight, it becomes evident that Stockton sacrificed its downtown for the war effort. A flood of environmental and social degradation spread from the channel, the source that had given it life 100 years earlier. But all cities undergo cycles of growth, stasis, decay and, hopefully, rebirth. They require vision, creativity, and management.

Photographs of the evolving urban landscape in Stockton from 1850 to 1950 populate this book. They provide vignettes of Stockton: how the city looked, where people married, worshipped, banked, shopped, and traveled. I have found the photographic record of Stockton revealing and sobering. It evokes a profound appreciation of the pioneer vision and sheer determination it took to create and sustain this city. The record also elicits questions about Stockton's history. But, most importantly, it contributes to a more informed view on the history of downtown Stockton and the challenges currently facing our city as we build its future. I have provided coordinates for many of the building locations so that this book can also function as an architectural tour guide to the city. In the end, I leave the reader with a report from the historical epicenter of the city, assuring you that Stockton is alive, well, and at the threshold of an urban renaissance.

WILLIAM M. STUART'S AMBROTYPE AND PHOTOGRAPH GALLERY, 1868. Stuart immigrated to Stockton in 1861 from Maine. He operated from three locations in Stockton between 1861 and 1872. Stuart's second studio, on the southwest corner of Hunter Street and Weber Avenue, was photographed by Lawrence and Houseworth in 1868. This studio burned shortly afterwards and he relocated to 198 Main Street.

One

LOCAL PHOTOGRAPHERS

Between 1850 and 1950, eight important photographers recorded the early settlement and spectacular rise of Stockton, from a rough, gold rush depot to a major Californian metropolis. Their extraordinary images document an odyssey of pioneers who, detouring from the gold trail, settled and built their fortunes in Stockton. The earliest of the eight, Benjamin P. Batchelder and Isaac S. Locke began working in mobile Daguerreian cars strategically located near the navigational headwaters of the Stockton Channel. By the 1860s, photography had become sufficiently profitable for the photographers to open their own indoor galleries. Within these relatively secure spaces, the photographers were able to store their negatives, thus establishing the archives and insuring the survival of Stockton's pictorial history.

By today's standards, the working conditions for these early photographers were deplorable. From 1859 to 1900, Locke, Batchelder, William Stuart, and J. Pitcher Spooner routinely used toxic chemicals in poorly ventilated, close quarters, sensitizing, exposing, and developing photographic wet plates on location throughout the growing city. Winter rains and tule fog limited access to locations and studios where available light was needed. These harsh working conditions quickly eliminated the less skilled photographers.

The momentum of Stockton's civic and commercial development provided cause and content for the photographers' work. Their images reveal what was important to the city's early settlers. Judging from the vast numbers of surviving photographic portraits of its inhabitants, portraiture was quite lucrative work. But considerable attention, encouraged by the advent of tourism and stereo photography, was given to the creation of urban views. During Stockton's first century, comprehensive photographic views of newly constructed buildings were frequently commissioned to serve as ceremonial records. Tragically, most of the earliest images of Stockton were lost when I.S. Locke's Daguerreian car was consumed by fire. Today, no more than eight views of Stockton from the 1850s are known to exist.

J. Pitcher Spooner was Stockton's first, truly systematic, documentary photographer. V. Covert Martin, beginning his career in 1900 as Spooner's career and life were ending, picked up Spooner's mantle. Spooner and Martin became documentary photographers by asking themselves the professional, if not always profitable question: what is worth recording for the future? Spooner's enterprise was inspired by his sense of history, his commitment to Stockton, and his willingness to speculate. He made a significant personal investment to document the streets and cultural institutions of Stockton. In a late interview, Spooner summarized the value he saw in his work, "It is true that I have never sold a single print from some of the best and biggest plates to the owners of the property, but I use them in other ways . . . and Stockton has been helped by it. It gives people a better idea of the place than could be obtained in any other way. People have been led to come to here and settle through my pictures." Although confident his photographs would become valuable in time, he did not realize a financially secure retirement from them, nor did he live to see the extent to which his work is appreciated today. V. Covert Martin had the luxury of learning from Spooner's life. Martin matured as a photographer under the guidance of Stockton photographer Charles Logan. He went on to produce commercial photographs and newspaper reportage for the *Stockton Record*. His photographs from 1920 to 1945 are an invaluable record of Stockton during its golden age. Upon his retirement, he began cataloging his collection of Stockton photographs (which included Spooner's work) and writing an illustrated history of the city. His career and life ended with acknowledgement of his work and in financial security.

ISAAC S. LOCKE, C. 1858. Locke worked as a mariner before immigrating to Stockton from Kentucky in 1856. He operated from a Daguerreian car on Main Street on the Courthouse Plaza in 1856 and 1866. Later he worked for William Stuart as a portrait photographer and colorist. Stockton's first historian, George Tinkham, noted that when Locke's Daguerreian car (studio) burned "hundreds of early views of Stockton were lost." However, several portraits of early Stocktonians made by Locke/Stuart have survived. Locke became a victim of Stockton's pioneer conditions. He died of dysentery in 1874 at age 50.

BENJAMIN AND NANCY BATCHELDER, BATCHELDER'S PHOTOGRAPHIC ART PLACE, C. 1890. The Batchelders worked together in Stockton from 1874 to 1893. During this period they published stereo photographs and operated the most successful portrait gallery in Stockton. Benjamin made the photographs and Sarah finished the photographs for sales.

JOHN PITCHER SPOONER, YOSEMITE THEATRE STUDIO, C. 1890. Spooner is Stockton's preeminent chronicler of the 19th century. He immigrated to San Francisco in 1863 and began his apprenticeship to William Herman Rulofson in 1865, opening his own Stockton Studio at 171 Main Street in 1870. Spooner created a large archive of stereo photographs and panoramic views of Stockton between 1870 and 1900 when Stockton was maturing as a city and poised for its golden era.

BATCHELDER'S PHOTOGRAPHIC ART PLACE, 183 EL DORADO STREET, c. 1874. Benjamin Batchelder purchased the Photographic Art Place from E.D. Ormbsy in 1874. Benjamin and brother Perez Batchelder were among the first photographers in Stockton, Sonora, and the southern Mother Lode region between 1852 and 1855. While in Stockton they worked from a mobile studio parked next to the Stockton House.

J. PITCHER SPOONER'S PHOTOGRAPHIC PARLOR, 171–175 MAIN STREET, c. 1878. J. Pitcher Spooner's first studio was located on the north side of Main Street between Center and Commerce Streets.

V. COVERT MARTIN, C. 1936. Van Covert Martin began his career (1900–1915) working for the commercial photographer Charles W. Logan. He then became the principle photographer for the *Stockton Record* newspaper (1915–1923) and was Stockton's principle photographer in the early half of the 20th century. He recorded Stockton as it matured to a vital California metropolis and through its golden era, from 1900 through 1945.

MARTIN STUDIO, 2317 PACIFIC AVENUE, 1937. V. Covert Martin's first two studios were destroyed by fire. He built his last studio on Stockton's Miracle Mile as the city began expanding to the north. He worked from this studio until his retirement in 1945. His archives were moved to the University of the Pacific in 1961.

13

CHARLES DAVID MARIA WEBER, 1850. Charles M. Weber was the principle founder and visionary for Stockton's future. This photograph is most likely his wedding portrait. Weber immigrated to California with the Bidwell-Bartelson party in 1841. Weber purchased the Spanish land grant El Campo de los Franceses in 1845. By 1848 Weber's vision for Stockton was drawn and under development.

HELEN MURPHY WEBER, 1850. Helen Murphy immigrated to California from Missouri with the Stevens-Murphy party in 1844. This is most likely her wedding portrait. With her father she settled in Santa Clara, where she met and married Charles Weber. With her marriage to Charles the couple moved to Stockton to live in the Weber home on the "peninsula."

Two

THE PIONEER'S VISION

Stockton became an incorporated city in 1850. Stabilized settlement began in 1847 when Stockton's founder, Charles M. Weber, acquired an 1843 Spanish land grant—Rancho Campo de los Franceses. This location attracted French trappers earlier in the century. Charles and Helen Murphy-Weber maintained a modestly scaled, lavishly furnished home on what is today Weber Point. The Weber home was surrounded by spectacular gardens that inspired city planning and visitors to Stockton. The Webers immigrated to California, Charles with the Bidwell-Bartleson party (1841) and Helen with the Stevens-Murphy-Townsend party (1844). The Weber's vision for Stockton was civic minded. Both had immigrated to California seeking opportunity, education, and religious freedom. They guided their vision with generous allowances for city parks and donated valuable lots to build churches and temples, schools, and civic buildings. Weber resisted efforts toward uncontrolled growth and destruction of the surrounding oak savannas.

The 1849 survey/plan for Stockton shows how Stockton began, as a grid of streets drawn over a natural system of sloughs and islands. Stockton was little more than a tent encampment and supply depot surrounding the head of navigation for the Stockton Channel. At that time Levee (Weber) Avenue, El Dorado Avenue, Main and Commerce Streets bound the early hub of commercial activity (1849–1855). Early residential districts formed to the southwest and north of the Stockton Channel. Stockton's urban development was accompanied by a re-engineering of the natural landscape truncating the waterways that once flowed through the original settlement. Today, following the advent of flood control these waterways might have been preserved to provide an extraordinary opportunity for development. During Stockton's early history these waterways were phantoms that swelled with seasonal rain and inundated the city. The same forces that produced such abundance also produced substantial hardship and loss.

Abundance and adversity became Stockton's muses prompting improved city planning. From 1855 to 1900, after a procession of devastating fires and floods, downtown Stockton migrated eastward. The courthouse provided a new identity. Fire-safe brick buildings and zoning produced commercial and culture corridors leading from the Courthouse Plaza in all directions. Weber continued to invest his personal fortune in flood control and other measures to stabilize progress for Stockton's city plan.

Weber's vision for a modern Stockton was achieved in relatively large increments. From 1860 to 1880 Stockton was a portrait of provincial harmony: courthouse, churches, schools, and homes sprouted from the plains in close proximity. The area surrounding the intersection of Main and San Joaquin Streets has been an ideal place to observe Stockton's urban evolution. This location has been a barometer for Stockton's civic, cultural, and commercial identity and priorities. By 1925 Stockton became a mature American metropolis.

Stockton optimized its strategic geographic location at the crossroads of California with the development of an urban public transportation system (1875), exchanging passengers and freight between steamships on its west side and railroad systems on its east side. Electricity was fully integrated in Stockton by 1892; the Stockton Electric Rail Road was created and survived until 1941. Steamship and rail travel stimulated a host of luxury hotels, reputable theatres, and public baths. By 1900 Stockton had become a California mecca for entertainment and recreation, the epitome of a sylvan lifestyle and the good life.

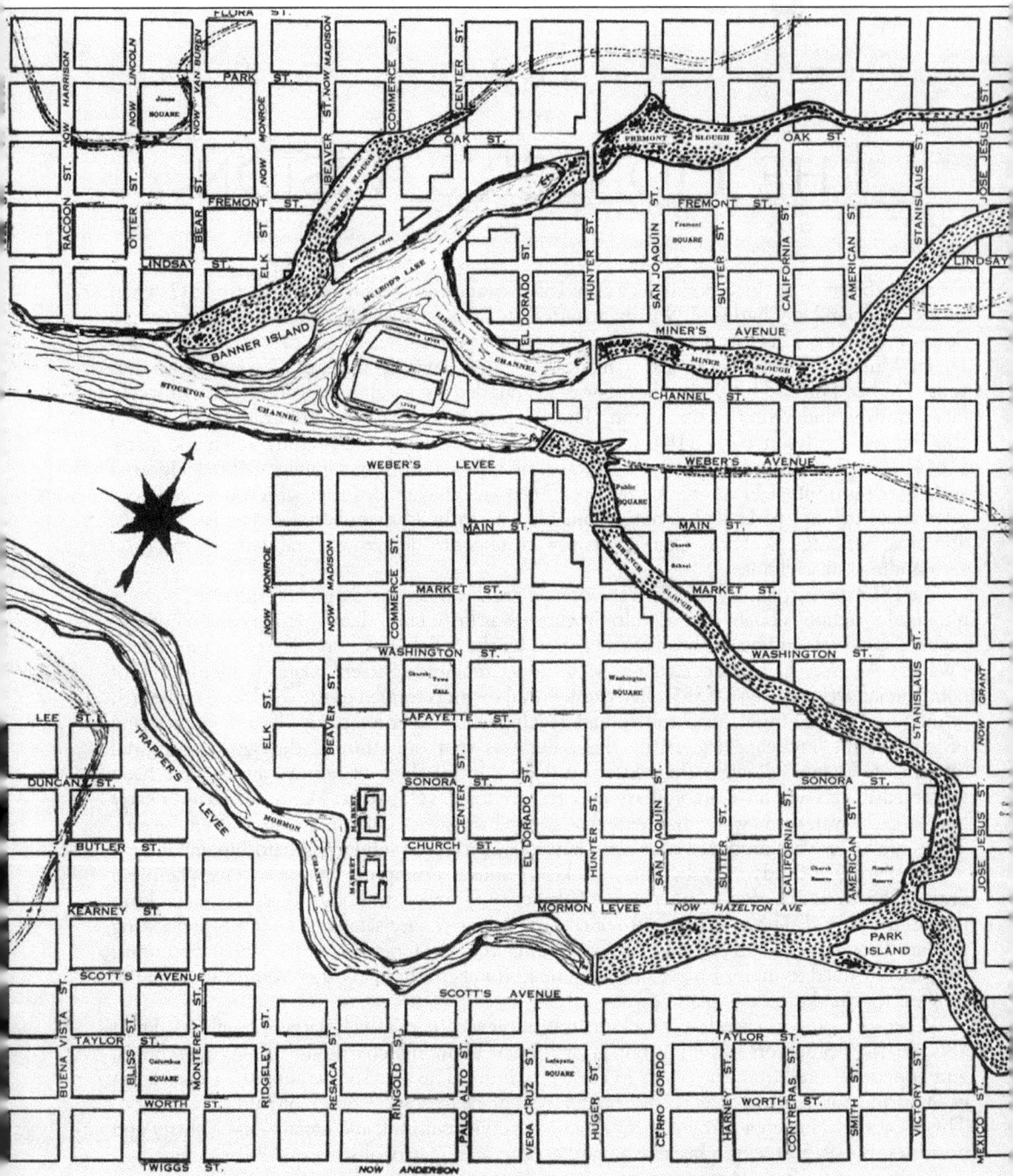

MAP OF STOCKTON, 1849. Stockton was surveyed and mapped at least twice in its formative years. This map, produced by Maj. Richard Hammond, reveals the plan for Stockton, a modern, gridded city crossing a natural system of sloughs that drained into the Stockton Channel. The waterways were truncated and "reclaimed" as the city grew.

WEBER HOME AND SLOOP MARIA, JULY 4, 1856. The Weber home, recorded as the first permanent home in San Joaquin County, was located on the peninsula, today's Weber Point. The Weber Home and Weber Point where it stood are considered to be the "epicenter" of Stockton. This house was built from native adobe, imported brick, and wood. The *Maria* was Stockton's first cargo ship.

HEAD OF NAVIGATION, STOCKTON CHANNEL, DECEMBER 1851. This view, looking southwest from today's Bridge and El Dorado Streets, records Stockton's first fire station (small building in the foreground), which remained here until 1852 when it was nearly swept away by a flood. This is the current location of Hotel Stockton.

C.M. WEBER'S STEAMER *SAGAMORE*, OCTOBER 1851. This view looks south to the intersection of Levee and Commerce Streets where ships unloaded cargo. The *Sagamore* was launched on its run to San Francisco in October 1851. On November 1, overloaded with freight and passengers returning to Stockton, it was destroyed by a boiler explosion. Important pioneer businesses are visible in the photograph. Stockton's first newspaper, the *Stockton Journal*, is located in the third building left of the intersection.

HEAD OF NAVIGATION, STOCKTON CHANNEL, OCTOBER 1851. The development of Stockton's downtown business district began near the head of navigation bounded by Hunter, El Dorado, Levee, and Channel Streets. This image shows Stockton's business district recovered from the December 1849 fire that destroyed most of the city along the south shore of the channel and only months before it was razed again.

CORINTHIAN BUILDING, OCTOBER 1851. Charles Weber and Richard Hammond constructed the Corinthian Building in the fall of 1850 along Stockton's north shore between El Dorado and Center Streets. The building functioned as Stockton's stagecoach depot, town meeting hall, theatre, and restaurant. The Angelo House, New York Hotel, and other early businesses are visible in the photograph.

ST. CHARLES HOTEL, 1854. The St. Charles was originally built as the Stockton House in 1849 on Channel Street between El Dorado and Hunter Streets. This photograph commemorates its new ownership and reopening as the St. Charles in 1854, shortly after the El Dorado Street Bridge was built. A cupola was later added to the building. Stockton's first theatrical performances and ball occurred here in March 1850. The St. Charles was destroyed by fire November 1871.

AVERY & HEWLETT, 1851. Following the devastating fire of May 1851, Stockton's business district began to migrate east toward the Courthouse Plaza and Main Street. Avery & Hewlett was one of several grocery and general provision depots that came to life in Stockton. Avery & Hewlett Grocery was located on the northwest corner of Main and Hunter Streets.

BIRD'S SADDLE & HARNESS DEPOT, C. 1852. M.L. Bird immigrated to Stockton in July 1850 from Middlebury, Vermont. He opened his first saddle and harness shop on Main Street between San Joaquin and Hunter Streets. Bird was one Stockton's early fire chiefs. He also introduced significant innovations to the horse collar that were adapted by fire departments across the country.

E.S. HOLDEN, C. 1865. Erasmus S. Holden immigrated to Stockton in 1849. Next to Charles Weber, he is considered the most influential pioneer to guide Stockton to stability and civility. He operated pioneer drug stores in Stockton and Sonora. After losing his store to the 1851 fire, he eventually established a fire safe store on the northeast corner of Main and El Dorado Streets. Among his contributions to Stockton's development, he was elected mayor six times, president of the Copperopolis Railroad, founding member of the Agricultural Society, and president of the San Joaquin County Fair Board.

SAN JOAQUIN COUNTY PIONEERS, C. 1878. The Society of Pioneers held annual picnics in Goodwater Grove, now Oak Park. From left to right are (front row) Ross C. Sargent, John Gratten, John C. White, Amos Gobe, and unidentified; (back row) William White, Jonathan Dodge, unidentified, M.P. Henderson, B.F. Sanders, William McKee Carson, Sylvester Tredway, and L.U. Shippee.

SAN JOAQUIN HALL OF PIONEERS, 1891. The Society of Pioneers was established in 1868. The first Hall of Pioneers was erected in 1890 on the northwest corner of Weber Avenue and Sutter Street. The archives and commemoration to the pioneers survives to this day in the Haggin Museum.

HAGGIN PIONEER MUSEUM AND GALLERIES, 1931. The successor to the Hall of Pioneers is the Haggin Museum, which opened in 1931 as the San Joaquin Pioneer and Historical Society. The Haggin was created for the preservation of local history. An art gallery and extraordinary collection of paintings from the collection of Louis Terah Haggin were added. The Haggin is Stockton's most comprehensive archive and accessible window to the city's history.

E.E. WASHBURN RESIDENCE, C. 1889. The E.E. Washburn residence was located on the north of the Stockton Channel. Electricity came to Stockton homes in 1888–1889.

STOCKTON RESIDENCE, C. 1888. A significant number of Stockton's early residents lived in boarding houses from 1850 to 1870. The average "middle-class" home was of modest design and constructed for the seasonal conditions of the Central Valley. This house was built south of Main Street. Elevated piers were used to minimize damage during the seasonal floods.

SAN JOAQUIN COUNTY COURTHOUSE, WINTER 1862. The county courthouse was the centerpiece of Stockton civic pride in the 19th century. Three courthouses have been built in Stockton since the first cornerstone was laid on August 6, 1853. The first courthouse was built in the neo-classical, Doric style. Its design influenced several civic buildings in Stockton from 1850 to 1870. Its location was debated from its inception. Charles Weber donated the land for the courthouse. Two sloughs flowing through the site were filled to prepare for construction.

EL DORADO AND LEVEE STREETS, LOOKING SOUTH, OCTOBER 1851. The core of Stockton's earliest downtown district was bound by El Dorado, Levee, Commerce, and Main Streets. Stockton's first post office was located in the Buffum and Cook store, the second building left of the intersection. This view shows Stockton recently recovered from its second devastating fire of May 1851.

MAIN AND SAN JOAQUIN STREETS, 1868. This intersection, viewed from the cupola of the courthouse may well be Stockton's symbolic terrain. It records the close proximity of Stockton's cultural and community institutions between 1860 and 1880. At this intersection you can see the Presbyterian church, Lafayette School, H.O. Mathews Grocer, J.P. Wilkin's Justice of the Peace, and the Main Street Livery. All of this is closely surrounded by private residence.

COMMERCIAL LOCATION MAP OF STOCKTON, 1875.

MAIN AND SAN JOAQUIN STREET, C. 1900. By 1900 Main Street had reinvented itself from its pioneer foundations. The wooden frame building in downtown Stockton became history.

MAIN AND SAN JOAQUIN STREET, C. 1925. Twenty-five years later the intersection of San Joaquin and Main Streets is transformed from the pioneer vernacular and intimate scale to the robust, with a modern skyscraper becoming a snapshot of downtown Stockton's golden era. The influence of Beaux Arts, revivalist architectural style, was used extensively by Stockton architects during the early decades of the 20th century.

STOCKTON STREET RAILROAD COMPANY, C. 1889. The Stockton street car system was established in 1875 using four cars built in San Francisco. This photograph records an enclosed winter car turning north and passing by the Holden's Drug Store on the corner of Main and El Dorado Streets. Built in 1851, Holden's Drug Store was an important Stockton landmark that survived into the 1960s.

STOCKTON STREET RAILROAD COMPANY, C. 1890. The horse stables were located on East Main Street between American and Stanislaus Streets where this photograph of a summer car was made. The horse-drawn era of public transportation ended in 1892 with the introduction of 10 horsepower electric cars.

DELTA KING AND DELTA QUEEN, 1941. The steamship trade, and rivalries, along the San Joaquin River highlights Stockton's history and brought significant trade and tourism. The *Delta Queen* and *Delta King* were constructed in Stockton in 1925–1926. Their appearance marks the zenith for large steamers in the Stockton Channel, punctuating the desire to dredge and create a modern port in Stockton. Both steamers were drafted as transports during World War II.

SOUTHERN PACIFIC RAILROAD, C. 1898. The last days of passenger service into the downtown area are recorded in this photograph of Weber Avenue between Hunter and San Joaquin Streets. In 1888, the Southern Pacific Railroad purchased the Copperopolis Railroad and operated its tracks on Weber Avenue for passenger, freight, and excursion trains until 1901. The terminal was then moved east to Sacramento Street.

STOCKTON ELECTRIC RAILROAD STREET CAR, C. 1930. By the 1930s all of Stockton's electric streetcar companies were purchased by Henry H. Huntington. This photograph shows a Birney Safety Car. Its route connected Goodwater Grove on the north of the city to the Municipal Baths on the south.

STOCKTON'S FIRST BUS SYSTEM, OCTOBER 1941. In 1939, W.I. Maxwell and the Stockton Chamber of Commerce proposed a study for the feasibility of converting the electric rail system to diesel engine buses. The Stockton City Lines placed five buses in service in 1941. The wire system and tracks of 1892 were removed.

STEAM-DRIVEN WATER PUMP, c. 1915. This photograph documents a steam-driven water pump in action at the corner of Weber Avenue and San Joaquin Street. The Stockton Fire Department was established in June 26, 1850.

FIRE AWARENESS PUBLIC PATROL VEHICLE, c. 1936. The history of Stockton has been profoundly shaped by fire. While casualties were minimized by an extraordinary fire department, the loss of property and employment because of fire was significant. Vehicles such as this were used to cruise the streets and in parades to heighten public awareness.

COMMERCIAL SAVINGS BANK FIRE, JULY 29, 1923. The Commercial Savings Bank fire began in the Philson Hotel and rapidly spread to the bank on the northwest corner of Main and Sutter Streets. One million dollars in damage was reported. The bank building was reconstructed and is still in service today as the Cort Building.

TAYLOR MILL FIRE, 1937. The Sperry Milling Company owned and operated the Taylor Milling Company. The Sperry Company was no stranger to fire. The first Sperry Flour Mill was completely destroyed by fire in April 1882.

HIGH WATER IN STOCKTON, 1862. The same forces that endowed Stockton with rich soils and abundant water were perennial threats to its progress. In February 1862, the Central Valley, from Bakersfield to San Francisco, became an inland sea for 14 days. This rare view of Stockton during the flood looks north from San Joaquin and Market Streets. When the floodwaters finally receded, Stockton was mired in "an impossible layer of black mud and sand."

MOTHER AND CHILDREN, WAITING OUT THE FLOOD, 1881. The flood of 1881 was not unusual for Stockton. Achieving a high watermark of four feet, the Mormon Slough and the San Joaquin breeched their banks and submerged the south side of the Stockton channel near Market and Monroe.

VIEW OF MINER AVENUE LOOKING EAST, MARCH 21, 1893. Another large flood inundated Stockton in winter of 1893. This view shows the attempt to minimize damage to the First Congregational Church located between San Joaquin and Sutter Streets. This photograph is part of a series of flood images produced by J. Pitcher Spooner.

FLOOD OF 1907, SECOND DAY. This photograph and handwritten note records Main Street Stockton looking west between Hunter and El Dorado Streets, March 9, 1907. This year, 12 boats were grounded at the confluence of Mormon Channel and tons of debris and silt were deposited everywhere. By this time several means to impose flood control were under consideration.

STOCKTON INDEPENDENT, C. 1875. At least 10 newspapers were published from Stockton between 1850 and 1930. The *Stockton Independent* published from 1861 to 1939. The *Independent*, with a strong Republican party position in favor of the North, entered Stockton's editorial climate, which was dominated by pro-Southern sentiment. The *Independent* was the first California newspaper to use linotype and steam power to run its presses.

EVENING HERALD, C. 1880. The *Evening Herald* was one of Stockton's short-lived newspapers, first published by William Biven in July 1865. By 1869 it was absorbed by the *Stockton Gazette*.

STOCKTON RECORD BUILDING, C. 1926. The *Record* was founded in 1888 as the *Commercial Record*. It became the *Stockton Record* in April 1895. The *Stockton Record* was founded by Irving Martin and William Denig as a small weekly sheet supported by advertising revenue. It eventually purchased its competitors, the *Evening Herald* and the *Evening Mail*, becoming Stockton's principal newspaper to date.

SAN JOAQUIN COUNTY COURTHOUSE, 1867. The county courthouse and surrounding plaza became a significant source of civic pride and the hub of downtown Stockton's commercial life. By 1870 the original courthouse had been upgraded with belfry, clock tower, mature landscape, and artesian fountain. This photograph was part of a stereo series on Stockton produced and published by the San Francisco photographer, Thomas Houseworth. The Agricultural Pavilion can be seen to the right of the courthouse.

Three

COMMUNITY
CORNERSTONES

A photograph cannot record civic and cultural pride, but judging from the number of photographs made of Stockton's civic and cultural institutions during the 19th century, it is evident Stocktonians were very proud of their city. The conspicuous disappearance of such photographs as the city progressed through the 20th century is puzzling. Great architecture can inspire amazement while buttressing a community's confidence and principles. Stockton produced its share of great buildings. Between 1850 and 1950 extraordinary civic buildings, schools, libraries, churches, temples, and hospitals were constructed. Many of these buildings remain in Stockton today, but most survive only as photographs.

Many fine photographs were devoted to the first two county courthouses whose histories parallel the fate of a number of Stockton's most beautiful buildings. The cornerstone for Stockton and San Joaquin County's first courthouse was laid in 1853. That stone anchored the community, launching Stockton on a marvelous course of accomplishment its pioneers could not have entirely imagined. The courthouse served double duty as legal center and as a ballroom when formality and sophistication was needed. It was a source of community pride and inspired a bid from city representatives to make Stockton the state capital. The cornerstone for Stockton's second courthouse was laid 45 years later. Two years in the making, this courthouse opened to an awestruck public who proclaimed it was "the finest Courthouse in the State." Its destruction in 1961 astonished and dispirited many Stocktonians, irrevocably changing the city.

Stockton's civic center was developed north of the Stockton Channel in the mid-1920s. Planning began with the city hall, a practical solution to overcrowding in the courthouse. Design had barely started when a deeply patriotic public voted in favor of a bond issue to construct the Stockton Civic Memorial Auditorium as a venerable expression and public monument to Stocktonians killed in World War I.

Diverse religious institutions have enjoyed prosperity in Stockton from its beginning. They have contributed many of the architectural accents and legacies to the community. Weber's founding vision for Stockton included a sanctuary and tolerance among diverse faiths. He supported this vision by granting all requests for property to construct churches or temples during his lifetime. His vision held, withstanding two brief harassments by the Ku Klux Klan. Today, Stockton is one of the most religiously diverse communities in the country.

Stockton public education produced a significant number of inspiring buildings. Guided by a visionary mayor, the public school system was established by common council and initially funded by private donations in 1852. It mirrored the prevailing egalitarian impulse of the country. Desegregation of socio-economic class began in the 19th century and race in the 20th. In the intervening 150 years, the school system has struggled to uphold the dream of a common educational experience by planning and remaining ahead of overcrowding, mitigating decay, and avoiding the demolition boom. Many of Stockton's early schools were retired, worn out and insufficient to the task. Others were prematurely razed, victims of the Field Act and subsequent legislation requiring seismic upgrades. By 1970, nearly all of the historical schools in Stockton were gone.

LAYING THE CORNERSTONE FOR A NEW COURTHOUSE, 1888. The extraordinary expansion of the county population and Stockton's industry prompted the replacement of a small and worn-out courthouse. On February 22, 1888, cornerstone ceremonies for a new courthouse were conducted by the Grand Lodge of Free Masons. The San Joaquin and Morning Star Lodges assisted.

VIEW OF THE COURTHOUSE, LOOKING NORTHEAST FROM HUNTER AND MAIN STREET, 1890. A superb example of the neo-classical style, the new courthouse was considered to be the finest of its kind in California. All of the materials used to construct it were produced locally and a special railroad spur was built from the Copperopolis line on Weber Avenue to deliver materials to the site.

STOCKTON SENDS GREETINGS, C. 1920.
The courthouse cupola was electrically
lighted for special holidays and occasions.
This photograph shows the Main Street
(south) side of the cupola.

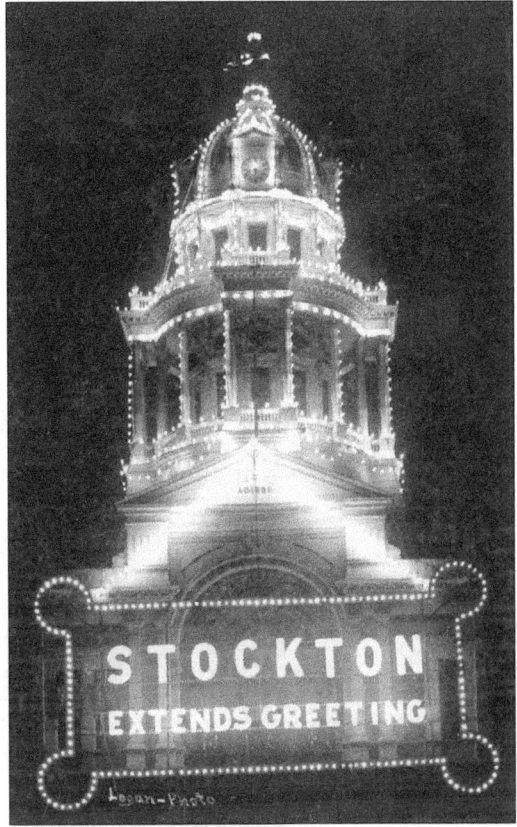

**DEMOLITION OF COURTHOUSE, AUGUST
1961.** The second San Joaquin County
Courthouse was finally brought down in
August 1961. Public support for its demise
was not unanimous. Stockton embraced
urban renewal programs during the 1960s
and the monuments of its golden era live
on mostly in photographs.

POST OFFICE, JULY 4, 1876. Stockton's main post office has been located in eight different locations between 1850 and 1934. This view documents the fourth location on the west side of the plaza. The building is decorated for national centennial.

POSTAL EMPLOYEES, C. 1880. From left to right are (front row) A.E. Eller, John S. Newman, and William Elsoy; (back row) George S. Pool, John Nuffy, William Whiting, and P.W. Burgess.

POST OFFICE, C. 1925. The seventh Stockton post office was built in 1902 on the southeast corner of Market and California Streets. It served Stockton until 1934.

POST OFFICE, 1933. The eighth Stockton post office was built on the northwest corner of San Joaquin and Lindsay Streets. Still in use, it is an excellent example of the 1930s Depression-era and Works Progress Administration (WPA) projects. The building was designed with allusions to a Federalist, Moderne style, accented with cubist-like elements. The interior features WPA murals.

STOCKTON CITY HALL, 1926. Stockton's civic center began to take shape in the mid-1920s with the construction of the city hall and the Civic Memorial Auditorium. The construction of Stockton's city hall was a response to overcrowding in the courthouse. This photograph shows the south elevation on December 2, 1926.

VIEW OF CIVIC MEMORIAL AUDITORIUM, LOOKING NORTHWEST FROM CITY HALL, C. 1930. The Civic Memorial Auditorium represents a marriage of the practical need for a larger auditorium and a venerable expression and public monument to Stocktonians killed in World War I. In the months following the war, the auditorium was proposed as part of the civic center development north of the Stockton Channel at Fremont and Center Streets. When the auditorium was dedicated in November 1926 the street grid did not fragment the civic center as it does today. The placement of the auditorium produced a park-like blend of classically inspired architecture and the Fremont Channel, which reaches into the city from McLeod's Lake. In later years, Center Street was projected south and the waterway filled, having an immediately efficient yet anesthetic effect.

VIEW OF AUDITORIUM, LOOKING SOUTHWEST FROM CENTER AND OAK STREETS, 1926.
Stockton architects Glenn Allen, W.J. Wright, and Ivan Satterlee orchestrated the design of this classically inspired building. The project was financed through a bond and construction commenced in 1925 under the supervision of Frank Tucker. Sculptor Joseph Wicks added the final touches with relief sculptures for the frieze and over the foyer doors.

INTERIOR VIEW OF STOCKTON MEMORIAL CIVIC AUDITORIUM, 1926.

STOCKTON POLICE, 1884. From left to right are (front row) Tom Towell, Riley Wells, Nap Edwards, Mike Finnell, and William B. Wollan; (back row) Sidney Ralf, Farn Mc Cloud, D. McKinnon, J. Rhoder, J. Williams, and C. Beckhart.

SAN JOAQUIN COUNTY AND STOCKTON CITY JAIL, C. 1880. The early Stockton jails were miserable, located in the hull of the brig *Suzanne* and later in the damp basement of the McNish building. The alternative was frontier justice, i.e., the vigilance committees. In 1853, the first Stockton jail was constructed on Market Street between Hunter and San Joaquin Streets. Before the state prison system was constructed, Stockton's jail was called upon to hold prisoners from several counties. Overcrowding was the result.

TRAFFIC OFFICER J. SHOEMAKER, 1922. This photograph was made outside the Western Pacific Railroad Depot in 1922. Shoemaker had recently joined the department.

SAN JOAQUIN COUNTY JAIL, C. 1893. By 1890, a full-time jail staff was required and chain gangs were introduced to relieve the overcrowded conditions of the jail. A new county jail was constructed on the northwest corner of San Joaquin and Channel Streets. It was affectionately dubbed "Cunningham's Castle" for the county sheriff of the day. The "Castle" was designed to accommodate 75 inmates. In 1959, the county jail was relocated to new facilities in French Camp, south of Stockton.

DR. DAMERON AND NURSING STAFF, C. 1915. John Dysart Dameron, M.D., arrived in Stockton in 1895 and established the Dameron Hospital shortly thereafter at 1049 North Lincoln Street. He also provided distinguished service as a county health officer. In 1915 Dameron built a new hospital, which was later purchased by a local physicians' group. The hospital continues as a vital part of the community today.

STOCKTON STATE HOSPITAL, C. 1940. Human disappointment and misfortune were added to the tailings of California's Gold Rush. Medical care and hospitals of any sort were rare. County governments inherited Gold Rush indigents. On March 26, 1851 the state legislature initiated actions to create a state hospital system. By 1852 the formation of the Stockton State General Hospital and Asylum for the Mentally Insane was under way and patients were being received. The Stockton State Hospital served many communities throughout the state. In the aftermath of the 1906 San Francisco earthquake, Stockton received 99 survivors from the destruction inflicted upon St. Agnew's Hospital near San Jose. By the mid-1950s, the Stockton State Hospital cared for 4,600 patients.

MEDICO-DENTAL BUILDING,
c. 1930. The Medico-Dental
Building was built as Stockton's
first professional medical
building, consolidating private
practice medical services for
the community. It was designed
and built by Frank V. Mayo and
Howard Bissell in 1926–1927. A
beacon on the urban landscape, it
is the tallest building in Stockton.

ST. JOSEPH'S HOSPITAL, C. 1930. Stockton's oldest private hospital, St. Joseph's Hospital was established by Fr. W.B. O'Connor in 1899. The founding order and staff of St. Joseph's was Dominican. Today it prospers as a non-sectarian institution.

MIDNIGHT MISSION, C. 1936. The Midnight Mission is one of many efforts made by Stockton's diverse charitable communities committed to helping the unfortunate. The Midnight Mission provided food and shelter for the homeless and the unemployed during the Great Depression of the 1930s.

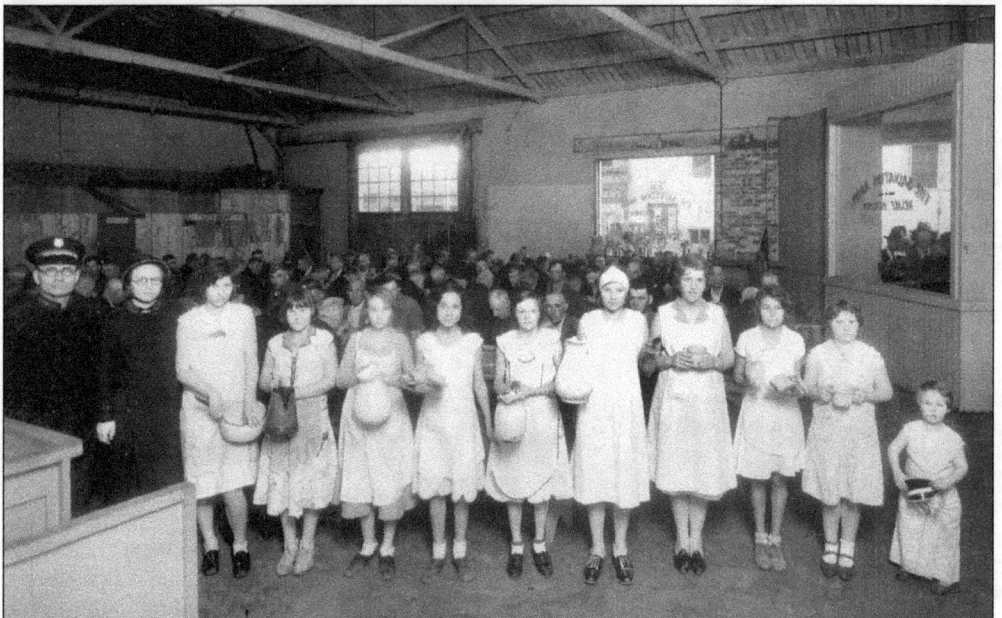

SALVATION ARMY RELIEF KITCHEN VOLUNTEERS, C. 1932. For all its distinctions, Stockton shares with all cities individual stories of tragedy and despair. Seasonal agriculture and economic famine often produce a population of disenfranchised and homeless. The Salvation Army operated a relief kitchen at 301 South Sutter Street.

ODD FELLOWS HALL, C. 1874. The Stockton lodge of the Independent Order of Odd Fellows (IOOF) formally organized between 1850 and 1852. Fire evicted the Odd Fellows from their first lodge on Center Street in 1855. As they regrouped, the Odd Fellows assembled at the first public library in Stockton, and they built their first dedicated lodge on the southeast corner of Main and Hunter Streets in 1866.

MASONIC HALL, C. 1900. The Masonic Hall for the Free and Accepted Mason had its formal beginning in Stockton on May 5, 1852. In 1883 the Masons constructed their first dedicated hall on the old site of the St. Charles Hotel. The ground floor was rented to private businesses and the Masons occupied the auditorium and offices on the second and third floors. The building was demolished in 1933. The new Masonic Hall was designed by architect Carl Werner and constructed in 1921 on the southwest corner of Market and Sutter Streets. It is an example of Spanish Colonial Revivalist style with a Gladding McBean terracotta cornice and surround at the entry of the building. The hall survived a fire in 1949 and is well preserved today.

FRANKLIN GRAMMAR SCHOOL, C. 1890. Two Franklin school buildings were constructed and are visible in this photograph. The Franklin Primary School was Stockton's first public school building, constructed in 1859. Overcrowding prompted the construction of the Franklin Grammar School in 1872. The Franklin schools were designed in the Doric style and located on Center Street between Washington and Lafayette Streets. They were demolished in 1957.

LAFAYETTE SCHOOL, C. 1874. "Some kindly progressive citizen set fire to the structure" was George Tinkham's wry comment on the slow development of the Lafayette Grammar School between 1861 and 1865. The Lafayette School was finally constructed and opened to overcrowded conditions. Like other public schools in downtown Stockton, it was inundated with industrial noise and roaming livestock. The school provided the city's first coeducational curriculum.

WASHINGTON SCHOOL, C. 1895. The Washington School location served Stockton well. It began in 1867 as the Fremont Square School on the southeast corner of Lindsay and San Joaquin Streets. In 1869 it became the Washington Grammar School. A third floor was added in 1891 and the school began its life as Stockton High School. In 1915 and again in 1945 the building served various administrative functions for the county school district.

CLASS PORTRAIT FROM WASHINGTON HIGH SCHOOL, C. 1895.

WEBER PRIMARY SCHOOL, c. 1878. Weber Primary School, constructed in 1875, was named for Charles Weber, the founder of Stockton and its benefactor. (Weber donated nearly all public school properties in the downtown Stockton vicinity.) Stockton architect Charles Beasley designed Weber Primary School. Blending Italianate and Doric styles, the same plan was used to construct Franklin Grammar School. Today, Weber Primary School functions as an administrative building.

JEFFERSON SCHOOL. 1885. Jefferson School was constructed on the northwest corner of Weber Avenue and Pilgrim Street. It was built in 1871 in the French Second Empire style, a revival style popular in its time.

FREMONT GRAMMAR SCHOOL, COLUMBUS DAY, 1892. Fremont Grammar opened in 1890 to accommodate east side growth. The *Stockton Record* blasted the school board for approving its design, which it called "a miserable piece of botch work." The school was built over the filled Fremont slough. Prone to flooding and subsidence, it was permanently closed in 1941.

EL DORADO ELEMENTARY SCHOOL, 1898. El Dorado School was the first school in Stockton to take its name from its location rather than commemorate a president or famous individual. It was located on the north side of Vine Street between El Dorado and Center Streets. It was the first Stockton school to have indoor lavatories and running water. Short lived, it was demolished in 1915.

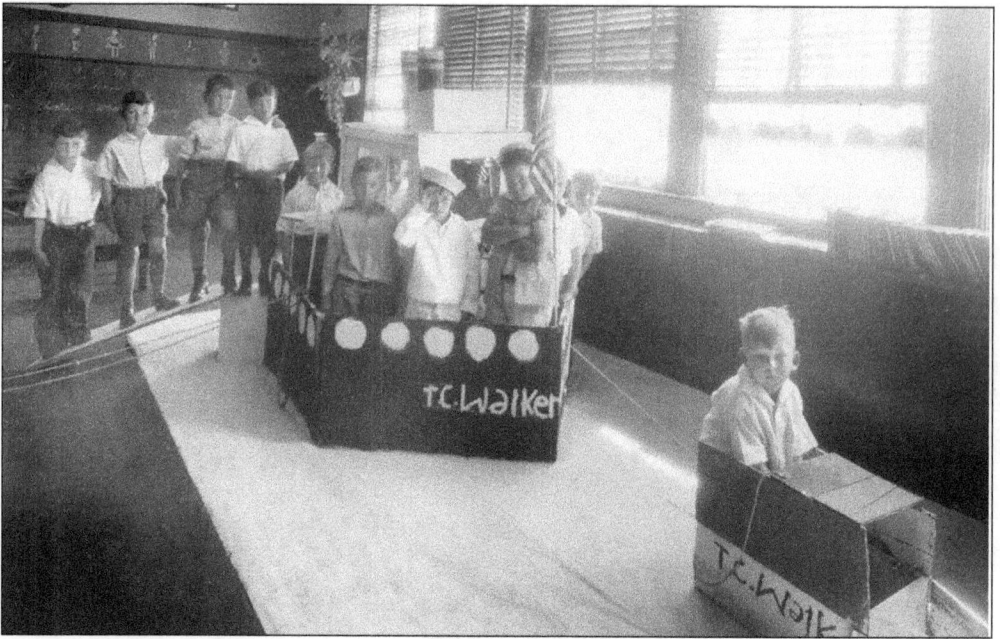

LOCAL HISTORY LESSON. This photograph from El Dorado Elementary School suggests the impact of local steamship legends on the classroom curriculum. Capt. T.C. Walker was the president of the California Steamship Company. Two steamships carried Walker's name.

EL DORADO GRAMMAR SCHOOL, C. 1920. The second El Dorado School was designed and built in 1915–1916 at the northern edge of Stockton's city limits. Anticipating growth, Stockton architects William J. Wright and Louis Stone designed the spacious El Dorado in the collegiate Gothic style. The building is still in use today.

STOCKTON HIGH SCHOOL, C. 1950. Stockton's first dedicated high school still looms large in the public memory. It produced a list of distinguished graduates and community leaders. Controversy accompanied development: location and architect were each contested. Stockton architect George Rushfaller designed the Stockton High School in the Anglo-Classic style. Overcoming a host of political and construction obstacles, the high school opened for instruction in 1904. The school received national attention in the educational journals of the time for design and curriculum.

THE COLLEGE OF THE PACIFIC, 1923. The College of the Pacific is California's first institution of higher learning, established in 1851 by Methodist pioneers. The college moved from Santa Clara to Stockton in 1923. The first classes were held in the *Stockton Record* building. Instruction on the new campus began September 24, 1924.

METHODIST CHURCH, C. 1863. The Methodist Church arrived in Stockton in the 1851. The original church building was located at Commerce and Washington Streets. This photograph is of the original building moved and remodeled on the northwest corner of San Joaquin Street and Weber Avenue.

METHODIST CHURCH AND CONGREGATION, C. 1878. The Methodist Church grew rapidly in Stockton. In 1870 they purchased the retired Agricultural Pavilion on San Joaquin Street between Weber Avenue and Main Street. In 1881 they built a new church on the northeast corner of San Joaquin and Miner Avenues. In 1958 they moved to Pacific Avenue and Fulton Street.

PRESBYTERIAN CHURCH, C. 1878. The Presbyterian Church arrived in Stockton in the 1851. The cornerstone for the new church was laid on June 10, 1859. Built in a Gothic Revival style, the church was located on the east side of San Joaquin Street between Main and Market Streets.

PRESBYTERIAN CHURCH, C. 1925. The new Presbyterian Church relocated to its present location on North El Dorado Street. The Presbyterians carried the Gothic Revival style with them, using architect Bertram G. Goodhue. The first services were held in the new church on Easter Sunday, 1923. The building remains in remarkable form today.

The Temple Israel was first erected in 1855 on Hunter Street near Lindsay Street. It was a modest wood frame structure built in the neo-classical vernacular style.

TEMPLE ISRAEL AND JEWISH COMMUNITY CENTER, 1930. Stockton's most famous architect, Glen Allen, designed the new Temple Israel in 1927–1928. Characteristically Allen, the temple and center were built in a revival style showing strong influences from the Romanesque. The temple is no long standing but the exterior of the community center is beautifully preserved today.

ST. JOHN'S EPISCOPAL
CHURCH, C. 1878.
The original St. John's
church was the first
brick and Gothic
Revival–style church
built in Stockton.
It was constructed
in 1857 on the
northeast corner of
El Dorado Street
and Miner Avenue
on land donated by
Charles Weber. The
old church building
was used until 1888.

ST. JOHN'S EPISCOPAL CHURCH, C. 1900. Plans for expansion of St. John's began in 1874. The Guild Hall was completed 1889, inspired by the Queen Anne style and drawings made by San Francisco architect Ernest Coxhead. Architect Walter King designed the new St. John's; the cornerstone was laid on April 14, 1892. St. John's is the third oldest Episcopal church on the west coast.

ST. MARY'S CATHOLIC CHURCH, C. 1865. The cornerstone for the original St. Mary's church was laid on July 21, 1861. The nave was designed by San Francisco architect William England in the Gothic Revival style popular for church construction of the period. St. Mary's survives as one of Stockton's oldest historic buildings. It is located on Washington Street between Hunter and San Joaquin Streets.

ST. MARY'S CATHOLIC CHURCH, c. 1893. St. Mary's building has been modified since it was first constructed in 1861. The bell tower was raised in 1893 but it remains true to the red brick, Gothic Revival style.

BAPTIST CHURCH, C. 1878. The Baptist Church dedicated its first church building on June 1, 1861. Built in the red brick Gothic style it was located on the southwest corner of Hunter and Lindsay Streets. Its towering steeple produced a noticeable landmark in early photographs of the Stockton.

SIKH TEMPLE, C. 1915. One of the little known facts about Stockton is that it was the first community in the United States to sanction a Sikh Temple, consistent with Weber's vision for religious freedom in this new California community. The Sikh Temple was constructed in 1915. The Sikhs joined a procession of immigrant agriculture workers to transform the reclaimed delta islands.

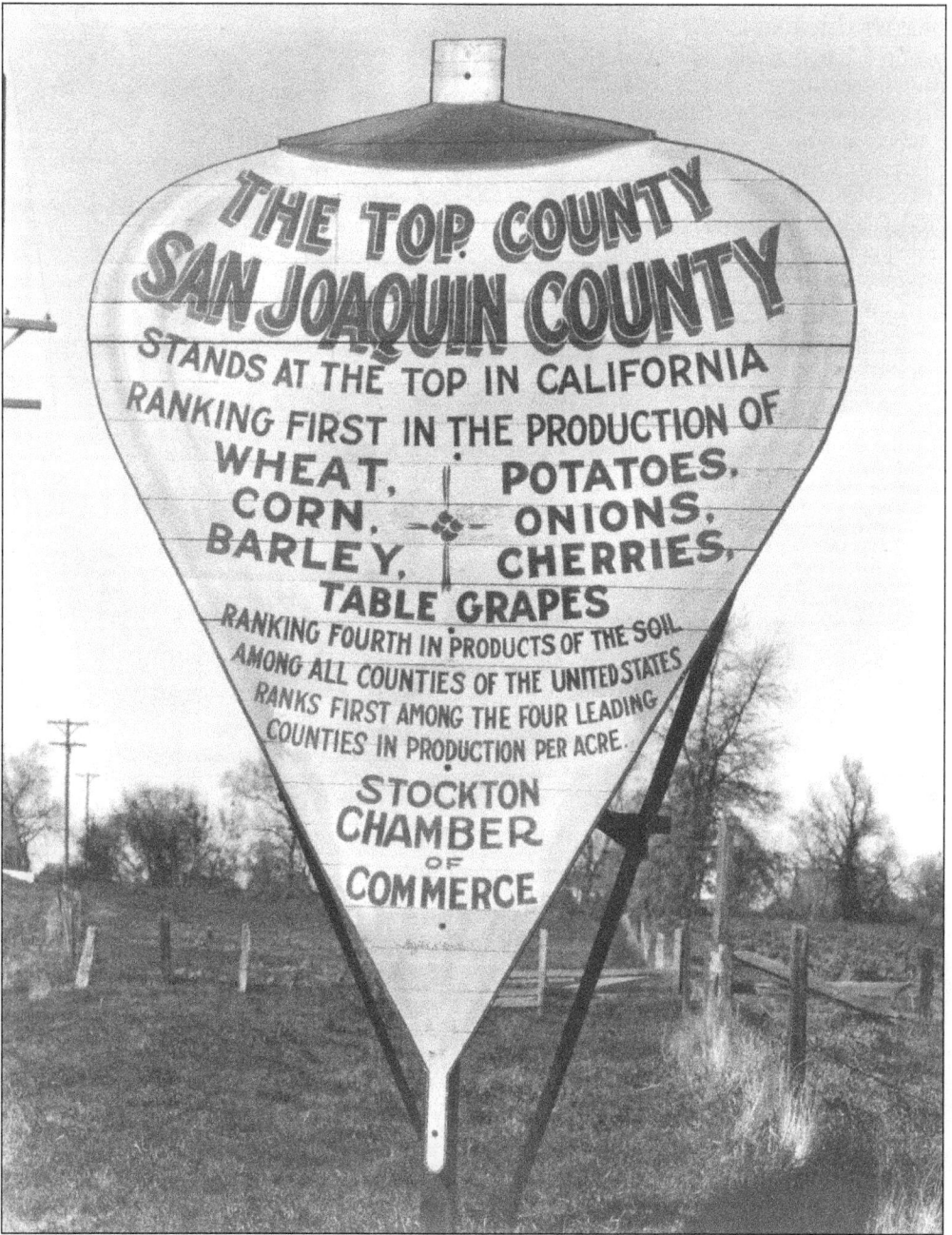

CHAMBER OF COMMERCE ROAD SIGN, C. 1926. Any way you spin it, in the wake of California's gold rush Stockton became an industrial and agricultural city from 1860 through the 20th century. Its influence was international. Every aspect of Stockton's economy and downtown district was touched by these influences. The industrial arts, re-engineering water and soil, and a port that filled breadbaskets and tables around the world defined the creative genius of Stocktonians.

Four

INDUSTRY AND
AGRICULTURE

Stockton is arguably the focal point of a green revolution that began in the United States between 1870 and 1900. This is the legacy of an extraordinary group of industrial artists, manufacturers, and merchants that worked in Stockton and tackled significant obstacles in agriculture and industry with creativity. In the process they sparked a sizeable economy, personal wealth, and a dynamic downtown Stockton. Adding these accomplishments to the region's Mediterranean climate, extraordinary soils, and abundant water, San Joaquin County became and has remained among the top agricultural counties in the nation for nearly a century. Stockton's industrial innovations and agricultural machines have been exported to international markets and been indelibly written into history.

Stockton's miraculous rise to world-class agricultural and manufacturing city was well timed with the changes and innovations in California agricultural during the late 19thand early 20th century. Dry farming and the wheat bonanza of the 1870s were transformed by changing water laws and the formation of irrigation districts in the late 1880s. Cereal crops were changed to specialty crops produced in rows and orchards. Early inventions from Stockton—the Stockton gang plow and the McCormick harvesters pulled by large teams of mules—were superceded by new developments from Stockton shops: first steam, then gasoline tractors propelling the Delta tule breaker, pulling the combined harvester and lifting the clam-shell dredge. The innovation and adaptation of advanced tractor technology, best known in the Holt Caterpillar tractor, enabled Herculean amounts of work to be accomplished. Reclamation districts "followed the plow," providing opportunities for immigrant laborers to contribute to the creation of an agricultural empire around Stockton.

The blacksmith's machine shop and metal foundry, the wheelwright and wagon manufactories, and wood planning mills became cooperative components in Stockton's industrial revolution. If Stockton needed it, Stockton craftsman made it or invented it! Matteson and Williamson, from a small shop on the northwest corner of Main and California Streets, manufactured dump carts used to construct the transcontinental railroad. Later they manufactured and exported the Harvest Queen harvester from the waterfront. The Stockton, Globe, Geiger, Sterling, and Monarch Iron Works poured, forged, and fabricated heavy metal parts and hardware, stoking the momentum of Stockton factories such as W.P. Miller, Henderson and Son's, and the Hickinbotham Brothers, each of them Stockton legends.

Food growers and processors are the least known part of Stockton's history. Austin Sperry's Snowdrift flour; George Shima, "The king of the potato market"; and Tillie Lewis, the "tomato queen," achieved fame and fortune from the bountiful harvest of Delta farmland surrounding Stockton. Linked to Stockton Wharves, they exported their brands from Stockton to kitchens around the world.

Stockton began its life as a strategically located supply depot. Its agricultural merchants became the conspicuous component of the agricultural and industrial revolution. Webster, Hewlett, Cain, and Shaw were well-known outlets to local, regional, and national markets. They supplied provisions, equipment, and tools, initially to miners and later to the growing population of farmers farming the fertile plains surrounding Stockton.

THIRTY-TWO HORSE–DRAWN HARVESTER, C. 1890. A short list of Stockton industrialists who turned their creative energy to agricultural production would include Matteson and Williamson, L.U. Shippee, Benjamin Holt, and R.J. Le Tourneau. The horse-drawn Stockton gang plow, California header, and McCormick thresher were manufactured in, used in, or widely exported from Stockton. Linking these machines to the steam engine and, later, the internal combustion engine was just around the corner.

STEAM TRACTION ENGINE, DELTA ISLANDS, WEST OF STOCKTON, C. 1906. As the 19th became the 20th century, the horse-drawn harvester became the steam tractor–drawn harvester. The Holt Brothers entered the market for steam tractors, adapting their wheel-making business to tractor design and the invention of the modern tractor, the Caterpillar.

HALF-YARD DITCHER, C. 1918. The endless combinations and improvements of machinery by Stockton inventors were adapted to undertake land reclamation for farming irrigation and for flood control in the Central Valley. The Half-Yard ditcher, which combined the Clam Shell dredge with the Caterpillar track, was created by the Stockton Iron Works, located on the north shore of the Stockton Channel.

DREDGING THE DEEP-WATER CHANNEL, C. 1920. As early as the 1870s a desire to deepen and straighten the Stockton Channel was investigated. Other projects reshaped Banner Island and the entrance to McLeod's lake. By 1931 the effort was finally supported by bond money and the modern port of Stockton began.

WILLIAM P. MILLER'S CARRIAGE MANUFACTORY, C. 1880. William Miller's saga is legendary among Stockton's stories. He immigrated to Stockton in 1851 and, in a short time, manufactured his first wagon under an oak tree. He is said to have used lumber and metals salvaged from abandoned ships in Mormon Slough. Miller became most famous for manufacturing the Stocktonian, a large-capacity freight wagon selling for $1,000.

M.P. HENDERSON AND SON CARRIAGE FACTORY, C. 1880. M.P. Henderson became famous for manufacturing the 20-mule team wagon that was used to haul borax from the mines of Death Valley. Henderson's factory was located on the northeast corner of Main and American Streets.

STOCKTON IRON WORKS, C. 1876. The Stockton Iron Works is Stockton's oldest continuously operating foundry and machine shop. It began operation in 1868 as Farrington, Hyatt and Co. As property in downtown Stockton became more valuable for retail office and residential hotel space, the foundry moved to the north side of the Stockton Channel, where it operates today.

POURING IRON, STOCKTON IRON WORKS, C. 1924. There were several foundries and metalworking enterprises operating in Stockton; the Globe, Monarch, Sterling, and Geiger Iron Works are a few of the memorable companies that have operated in Stockton. Their work supported local manufacturing and exported to other concerns.

BENJAMIN HOLT TESTING A STUMP PULLER, C. 1900. A creative and tireless inventor of agricultural machinery that led to the adoption of chain tread and the Caterpillar tractor, a name given by Charles Clements, Holt's company photographer, Benjamin Holt is arguably the most well-known agricultural industrialist in Stockton's history. He began his Stockton business in 1883 as the Holt Wheel Manufacturing Company.

BENJAMIN HOLT AND GENERAL SWINTON, 1918. In 1918 British general E.D. Swinton visited the Holt factory on Aurora Street in Stockton. While commending Holt workers for their wartime effort and as a segue to praising the invention of the Caterpillar tractor, he commented on the invention of the machine gun by Hirim Maxim. "So while you Yankees have the credit for inventing the disease against humanity you also have the credit for producing the cure."

HOLT CATERPILLAR FIFTEEN AND HEADER, C. 1922. Over time most technological inventions become smaller and more powerful. The Holt Caterpillar tractor was certainly no exception. The Holt Caterpillar Fifteen is a great example of small, efficient tractor design. This photograph was made when this tractor was a prototype being tested for mass production.

HOLT CATERPILLAR, "D" SERIES PROTOTYPE, C. 1938.

SPERRY FLOURING MILL, JULY 4, 1876. The Austin Sperry Flouring Mill began in Stockton, in 1852, producing 150 barrels of flour a day from wheat imported from Martinez, California. In the 1860s San Joaquin County wheat was discovered to produce outstanding baking flour. At that time Sperry purchased the Franklin Flour Mill on the southwest corner of Weber Avenue and Madison Street and increased production to 600 barrels daily. Sperry's Drifted Snow Flour became nationally famous. Sperry Mills was purchased by General Mills.

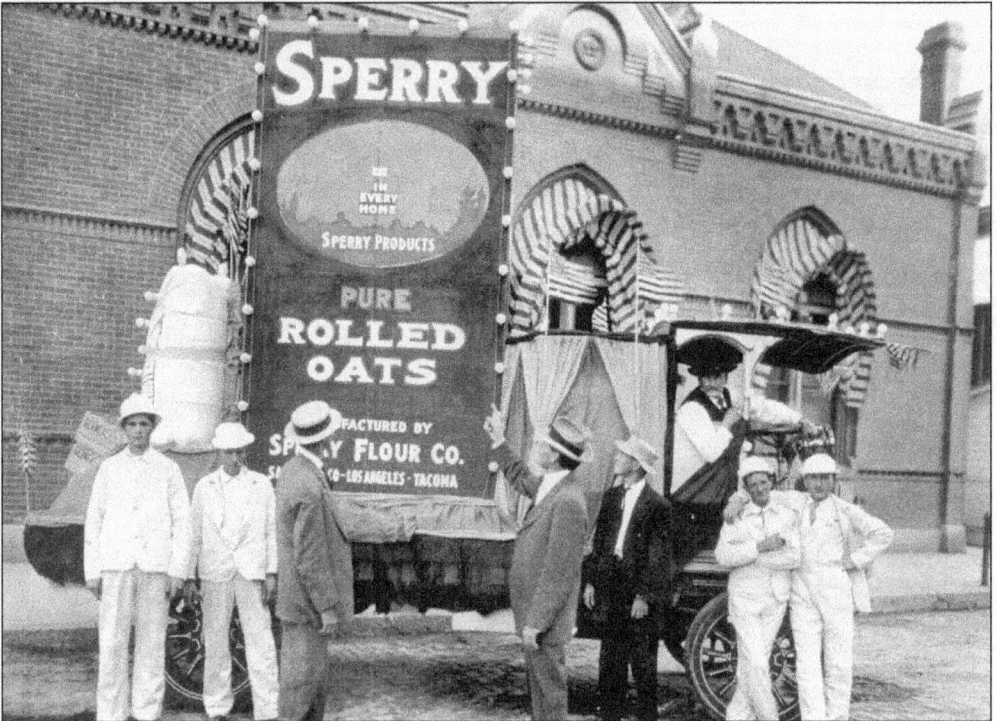

SPERRY ROLLED OATS, C. 1914. The Sperry Company also milled other San Joaquin County cereal grains from its Stockton mill. This photograph records a float being prepared for an Independence Day parade.

70

GEORGE SHIMA, SAN JOAQUIN COUNTY FAIRGROUNDS, C. 1918. Stockton was frequently called the "Holland of America" for its lowland peat soils. George Shima mastered farming them and gained an international reputation as the "King of the Potato Market." In 1908, Shima rented land, studied agriculture and marketing, and produced a fortune exporting his potatoes around the world.

TILLIE WEISBERG, C. 1950. Tillie Weisberg developed the multi-million dollar company Tillie Lewis Foods in Stockton from the idea that the Pomodoro tomato could be successfully grown and processed in California's Central Valley. The Tillie Lewis Cannery operated near the port of Stockton.

LOOKING WEST FROM INSIDE THE COPPEROPOLIS RAILROAD DEPOT, C. 1880. The Copperopolis Railroad Depot was constructed in 1869 to efficiently move large volumes of copper ore west from the foothill town of Copperopolis. The venture was poorly timed. The price of copper plummeted before the railroad was fully developed. It was eventually absorbed into the Central and Southern Pacific companies.

MARY GARRETT IN PORT, C. 1890. The *Mary Garrett* was built in Stockton, joining the California Steam and Navigation Company's fleet in 1878. The *Mary Garrett* and her sister ship, the *Alice Garrett*, operated among the many steamers that daily moved large volumes of grain and passengers between Stockton and San Francisco ports.

MATTESON AND WILLIAMSON, C. 1878. Matteson and Williamson opened their blacksmith shop at the northwest corner of Main and California Streets in 1852 from their shop. They manufactured iron machinery including dump carts for the construction of the Central Pacific Railroad.

EXPORTING THE HARVEST QUEEN FROM STOCKTON, C. 1890. The Matteson and Williamson Company produced the Harvest Queen, Harvest King, and Harvest Prince, some of the most famous harvesters to be exported from Stockton. The company began producing plows and harvesting equipment in 1852 from its shop at the northwest corner of Main and California Streets.

EXPORTING BRICKS FROM THE WATERFRONT, C. 1890. Virtually everything grown or manufactured in Stockton was exported from the Stockton Channel and wharves. Brick making is one of Stockton's least know and underappreciated early industries. Stockton bricks were used in hundreds of early San Francisco buildings.

JONES AND HEWLETT, C. 1870. The Jones and Hewlett Depot specialized in agriculture machinery. They were located on the northwest corner of Hunter and Main Streets on Courthouse Plaza. Earlier, the Webster Brothers, and, later, H.C. Shaw and John Caine were among the successful hardware and machinery merchants in Stockton.

JOHN CAINE AGRICULTURAL IMPLEMENTS, C. 1880. John Caine was a diversified businessman. He operated the Globe Ironworks and manufactured the famous Stockton gangplow. His business was located on Parker's Alley between Hunter and El Dorado Streets. Caine sold the business to Josiah Caine in 1900 and the enterprise survived with diminishing success until 1932.

H.C. SHAW PLOW COMPANY, JULY 4, 1876. H.C. Shaw began his career in Stockton as clerk for the Paige & Webster Hardware Company, located on the southwest corner of El Dorado and Main Streets. He purchased the company and later moved the office and manufacturing business to Parker's Alley between Hunter and El Dorado Streets.

H.C. SHAW PLOW COMPANY, C. 1940. The H.C. Shaw Company moved to the southeast corner of Weber Avenue and California Street in 1905. They remained at this location until the 1950s.

HICKINBOTHAM BROTHERS, C. 1865. Edwin and John Hickinbotham arrived in Stockton from New York in 1851–1852. They operated a carriage manufacturing business from 1852 to 1871 and a carriage and lumber business from 1872 to 1890. John's sons steered the company's interests from wood materials to industrial hardware, welding supplies, and steel.

SUPPLY VESSEL, JUNE 1944. The third generation of Hickinbothams formed Hickinbotham Bros. Ltd. in 1931. During World War II the Hickinbotham Bros. Construction Division built landing barges, floating cranes, steel tugs, and supply vessels, like this 176-foot-long one, for the U.S. Army. The Hickinbotham Bros. is Stockton's oldest, continuously operated family business.

MAIN STREET STOCKTON, C. 1926. By the 1920s Stockton matured as an urban metropolis and sustained a commercial vitality that rivaled all West Coast cities. Stockton had achieved a reputation as a "show town" for its theatres and music and as a recreation destination for its luxury hotels and mineral baths. For a couple more decades Stockton savored this blend of cosmopolitan lifestyle with its rural and agrarian identity that germinated in the 1870s.

Five

MAIN STREET STOCKTON

Stockton's golden era occurred between 1900 and 1945. By that time downtown had reinvented itself from rough and dusty gold rush depot, to bucolic village, to a commercial center by day and "bright lights, big city" by night. Early in the era Stockton's pulse was taken from Main Street; anywhere between El Dorado Street and American Street would do. Main Street was Stockton's New York sampler. The courthouse, banks, theatres, retail shops and professional office space were squeezed into five city blocks. Off Main had its glamour too. Swanky residential hotels, public baths, nightclubs, and an assortment of tawdry venues balanced urban life for an ethnically and socio-economically diverse population that included an abundance of tourists. All of this was connected by a public transportation system that worked. Stockton was, by all accounts, a well-oiled machine.

The migration of Stockton's downtown from the south shore of the channel toward Main Street began abruptly in the mid-1850s. A series of devastating fires and a new courthouse and plaza encouraged a burst of new commercial buildings and a more civilized public life. Between 1860 and 1880 wood frame buildings surrounding the courthouse disappeared, replaced by "fire safe" buildings. The close proximity of commercial, civic, industrial, and cultural enclaves began to disappear too. Charles Weber, the city's founder, died in 1881. Two decades later a reasonable semblance of the modern city he had envision had taken shape. A cleaner, architecturally current, well-proportioned city was in place. The neo-classical style was Stockton's first architectural style. Neo-Gothic, Renaissance, Baroque, Victorian, and Queen Anne styles followed with rapid succession. The elemental quality of the Greek-Doric style, favored by Thomas Jefferson, symbolized rationalism, stability and civic pride—badly needed qualities in frontier cities. Stockton vaulted into the 20th century. By 1917 the Farmer's and Merchant's Bank, formerly a small brownstone dressed in Victorian trim, bolted upward and welcomed Stockton to the skyscraper era, introducing a list of revivalist styles that decorated the next generation of community buildings. On a clear winter day, Stockton's skyline was visible for at least 50 miles.

The great commercial buildings of Stockton's golden era were banks and hotels. The banks were tall and robust; the hotels were elegant and refined. The bank buildings are intact today, though several institutions have passed through them. Most of Stockton's great hotels are gone. Hotels and boarding houses were vital to Stockton from its beginning and several luxury hotels have operated in the city. In 1910 Hotel Stockton, a Mission Revival masterpiece, represented the zenith of this era. Retail stores were plentiful downtown. From 1920 to 1940 Stockton received a generic list of nationally franchised stores. The old-line pioneer stores, Holden's Drugs, Steinhardt's, and Yosemite Cash Store gave way to the merchandising and advertising skills of companies like Owl Drugs, J.C. Penney, and F.W. Woolworth.

Downtown Stockton's big buildings reflected the robust economy of the region but it was small business operators that provided the mortar for the big bricks. Bakers, butchers, grocers, waffle shops, lunch counters, and a host of other service providers were sprinkled around the city, nourishing and maintaining the daily routine in a self-determined, self-contained city. Downtown sparkled one last time during World War II, manufacturing for government defense contracts. After 1950 Main Street slowly became dormant, dried up by the relocation of retail shopping and victimized by urban renewal. Today, Stockton is stirring and undergoing revival of its downtown, as it always has, near the waterfront where it began.

LOOKING NORTH ON HUNTER STREET FROM MAIN, STOCKTON PLAZA, C. 1878. Stockton began as a city of small merchants along the waterfront of Stockton Channel. By the 1860s a significant number of merchants relocated to the west side of the plaza near the courthouse. Migration continued eastward along Weber Avenue and the Main and Market Street corridors in the years to come.

VIEW OF MAIN STREET, LOOKING EAST FROM HUNTER STREET, 1924. By the 1920s Stockton's pulse was taken from the Main Street corridor between El Dorado Street to the west and American Street to the east.

HART AND THRIFT, C. 1890. The Hart and Thrift was a general merchandise and hardware store located on the northeast corner of Weber Avenue and Sutter Street. The business developed from a partnership between George Hart, a successful grain dealer, and E.E. Thrift, an equally successful grocer. The store operated from the 1870s to the turn of the century.

YOSEMITE CASH STORE, C. 1900. This late career photograph by J. Pitcher Spooner looks north over the intersection of Weber Avenue and San Joaquin Street, summarizing in one frame about as much of an orderly, modern city that Charles Weber could have imagined for Stockton. Commerce, law and order, and religion were now aligned. The old pioneer frame house, represented by the Columbia House, was the past; the mass and solidity of brick became the future. Before the decade was complete, the Columbia House was razed and Stockton became known as the "brick city." South and east of this site, the first modern skyscrapers of Stockton were rising up from the ground.

WINDOW DISPLAY, STOCKTON DRY GOODS, C. 1940. Window displays in Stockton stores were for many years a consistent subject for V. Covert Martin's camera. They often became the subject for printed advertisements or lantern slides shown before the main feature and during intermission in the local theaters.

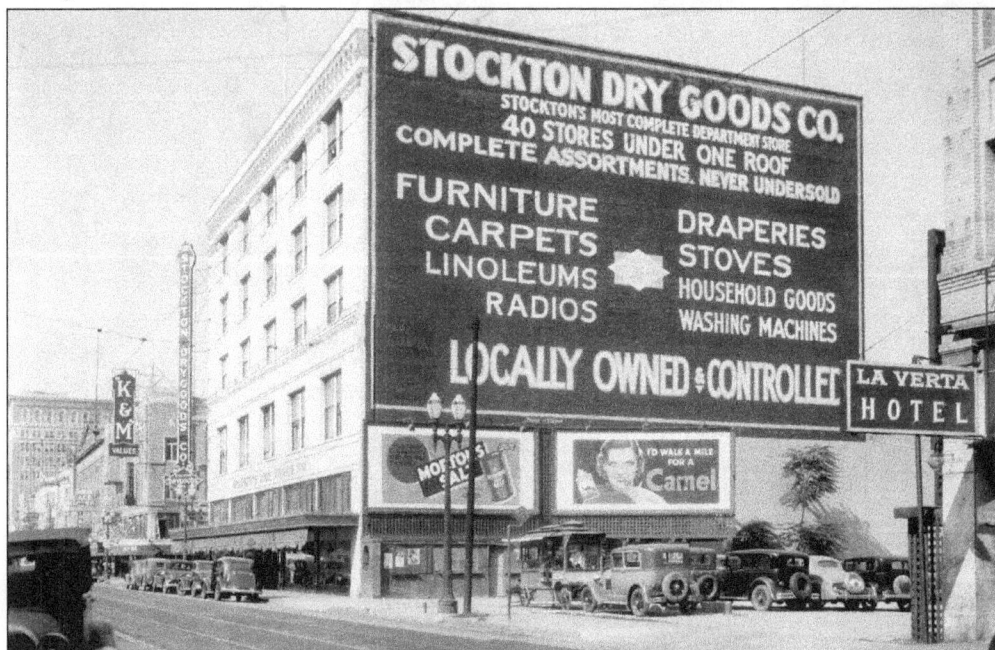

STOCKTON DRY GOODS, C. 1940. Originally located on the corner of Main and San Joaquin Streets, the Stockton Dry Goods store later stood at the northeast corner of Main and American Streets, the eastern end of Main Street's fashionable retail stretch. It was Stockton's largest locally owned department store, a greatly enlarged version of the Pioneer Provision Store.

STOCKTON SAVINGS AND LOAN SOCIETY, C. 1890. The first bank in Stockton was opened 1849, in a tent, by B. Walker Bours. It later became the San Joaquin Valley Bank. The Stockton Savings and Loan Society was founded in 1867. In the 1920s the Loan Society became the Bank of Stockton. The Bank of Stockton continues to operate today under its original charter.

STOCKTON SAVINGS AND LOAN BANK, C. 1922. The Stockton Savings and Loan Bank moved to Main Street in 1908 with the construction of Stockton's first skyscraper designed by San Francisco architects Meyers and Ward. The bank's design is inspired by the Renaissance Revivalist styles used by Chicago architect Louis Sullivan. The bank is located on the northeast corner of Main and San Joaquin Streets.

FARMERS AND MERCHANTS BANK, C. 1917. The Farmers and Merchants Bank, founded in Stockton in 1888, commissioned Stockton's third skyscraper. It was known in its day as the "bank of good service." The prominent San Francisco architect George W. Kelham designed the F&M Bank, inspired by the second renaissance and Grecian revival style; he also designed San Francisco's St. Francis Hotel. The bank wore several signs over the years, including United Bank and Trust, Bank of Italy, and Bank of America.

THE COMMERCIAL SAVINGS BANK, C. 1925. The Commercial Savings Bank building, designed in 1915, was Stockton's second skyscraper. This building survived a fire on July 29, 1923, and has managed to survive urban change. Today it is beautifully intact.

THE PHILADELPHIA HOUSE, C. 1878. The Philadelphia House was built in the early 1860s on the site of the Hotel de Mexico, an establishment built in 1849 by Col. Frank Cheatham. It became a sanctuary for Southern sympathizers as well as the locale of corrupt political dealings.

THE COLUMBIA HOUSE, C. 1878. The boardinghouse and hotel business was very important to Stockton's early history. The Columbia House was one of the earliest boardinghouses. Constructed from imported lumber, it first opened in the early 1850s as the Golden Lion Inn. In 1861, new owners renamed it the Columbia House. The structure was consumed by flames in the middle of the night of August 14, 1909.

THE MANSION HOUSE, C. 1874. The Mansion House was constructed in 1873 on the northeast corner of Weber Avenue and Hunter Street. It was the first large hotel near the courthouse. It later became the Windsor House. The original building is still in place, although the facade was remodeled in Moderne style.

THE IMPERIAL HOTEL, C. 1942. The Imperial Hotel on the southeast corner of Main and Aurora Street was constructed in 1897 and was Stockton's finest hotel until 1910. Featuring hot and cold running water, the Imperial attracted most of the celebrities performing at the Yosemite Theatre and distinguished guests visiting Stockton. It rebounded from fire in 1905. During remodeling in the 1940s, the Imperial gained exterior stucco and lost the top two floors.

THE HOTEL CLARK DINING ROOM, C. 1925. The Hotel Clark's dining room was distinguished by a series of Corinthian columns and was accented throughout with gold leaf.

THE HOTEL CLARK, C. 1925. The Hotel Clark opened in 1911. It was designed by Glenn Allen, Stockton's most imaginative and famous architect. In the 1920s, the Clark was one of the three classiest hotels in town, featuring a parking garage, dinner and dancing, and a pharmacy. The hotel was located on the southeast corner of Sutter and Market Streets where today is a public parking structure.

DINING ROOM, HOTEL STOCKTON, C. 1920. The Hotel Stockton was virtually self-contained. It offered boutique shopping, rooftop and interior dining, and lounges. The hotel's prospects dimmed during the post–World War II era, and it was eventually converted to a county administrative building. The Hotel Stockton is undergoing restoration at this time (2005) and many consider it a cornerstone for a renaissance in downtown Stockton.

THE HOTEL STOCKTON, C. 1920. Positioned at the head of navigation on the Stockton Channel, the Hotel Stockton was this city's grand statement to travelers for many years. It was designed by the architect Edgar B. Brown and has been cited as a "vast monument to Mission Revival Architecture." Construction was underway during the flood of 1909. It opened for business in 1910—the first steel reinforced concrete building in Stockton.

PROVISION STORE, STOCKTON, C. 1965. This provision store operated from the northeast corner of Levee (later Weber Avenue) and Hunter Streets, the Mansion House site. It sat just east of the head of navigation and at a significant intersection leading to the southern mines of the Mother Lode.

AVENUE MARKET, C. 1870. The Avenue Market operated from the northeast corner of Levee (later Weber Avenue) and American Streets. It served the east side of Stockton in its time and was known for its butcher shop. There were many independent grocers and butchers in Stockton, some more successful than others. City directories of the era list merchants such as Bluett Meat Market, South San Joaquin Meat market, and others.

FAMILY GROCERY
STORE, C. 1878.
The Black and
Brothers Family
Grocery Store was
located on the
northwest corner of
Center and Main
Street near the
large residential
district south and
west of Main and
Center Streets.

GRAVEM-INGLIS BAKERY, C. 1925. It is difficult to overstate the importance of the bakery
to Stockton in the 1850s. In 1851, William Inglis opened his first bakery on Center Street.
Stockton bakers used flour imported from Chile until it was discovered that San Joaquin wheat
milled to a superb baking flour. The Gravem and Inglis Bakeries consolidated two concerns as
one in the early 1900s.

HOLDEN'S DRUG STORE, c. 1874. Holden's Drug Company was organized by Erastus S. Holden in 1849. Rebounding from the fire of 1851, Holden built a fire-safe brick building on the northeast corner of El Dorado and Main Street. Holden's contributions to government and commerce distinguished him as one of Stockton's most important pioneers.

THE OWL DRUG COMPANY, c. 1925. The Owl Drug store began operating on the northeast corner of Main and California Street. Beginning in San Francisco in 1892, the Owl Drug Company franchised their stores across the country. They became famous for their soda fountains, pharmacies, and poisons packaged in distinctive, owl-shaped bottles. Owl Drug Company was purchased by Rexall Drug Company in 1930.

STOCKTON MILK COMPANY, 1925. In 1924, a typhoid outbreak occurred in Stockton. Many considered tainted milk to be the cause. This photograph is from an extensive series by V. Covert Martin featuring the production facilities of the Stockton Milk Company and demonstrating the sanitary conditions for all milk products cooperatively bottled in the plant.

BORDEN'S MILK DELIVERY, 1934. The Borden's Milk Delivery service began operating in Stockton in 1934. This photograph records their first fleet of delivery trucks purchased at the Althouse and Eagle Ford Dealership at 315 North El Dorado Street.

GLORIA ICE CREAM COMPANY, 1925. A city directory advertisement called it "the dish that never fails." The Gloria Ice Cream Company was the only one of its kind in Stockton when it arrived in 1917. Gloria was located on the southeast corner of Oak and Aurora Streets.

LIFE SAVERS PROMOTIONAL VEHICLE, C. 1936. This type of commercial advertising was widely popular through the late 1950s.

YOSEMITE CLOTHING HOUSE, C. 1874. The Yosemite Clothing House was constructed on the southwest corner of Main and San Joaquin Streets. It replaced the H.O. Mathews Grocery. The building remained at this location until the construction of the Farmers and Merchant's bank in 1916.

STEINHART'S IXL STORE, C. 1890. The IXL store for Men's clothing was another early specialty clothing store in Stockton. This photograph records the recent opening of Steinhart's new location on the northwest corner of El Dorado and Main Streets. Steinhart moved to the Hotel Stockton in 1910. The Batchelder's photographic studio can be seen on the right side of the photograph.

THE F.W. WOOLWORTH, C. 1918. In 1914, the F.W. Woolworth Company opened their first franchise in Stockton. The pioneering businesses of Stockton began to experience extreme competition from the emerging franchised stores such as Woolworth, J.C. Penney, and Owl Drugs. This Woolworth store was located at 422 East Main Street.

J.C. PENNEY DEPARTMENT STORE, C. 1936. J.C. Penney began operating in Stockton in the 1920s on Sutter Street. Their move to Main Street put them in the spotlight. This new location was formerly occupied by the Avon Theatre.

WINDOW DISPLAY, J.C. PENNEY, C. 1936. Window display photographs were routinely made for brochures and to be converted to lantern-slides for use in the theatres as pre-show and intermission advertisement.

WINDOW DISPLAY, J.C. PENNEY, C. 1936.

THE MODE O' DAY WOMEN'S APPAREL STORE, C. 1932. The Mode O' Day Store was among the many fashion boutiques located along Main Street Stockton. Mode O' Day operated in Stockton into the 1960s.

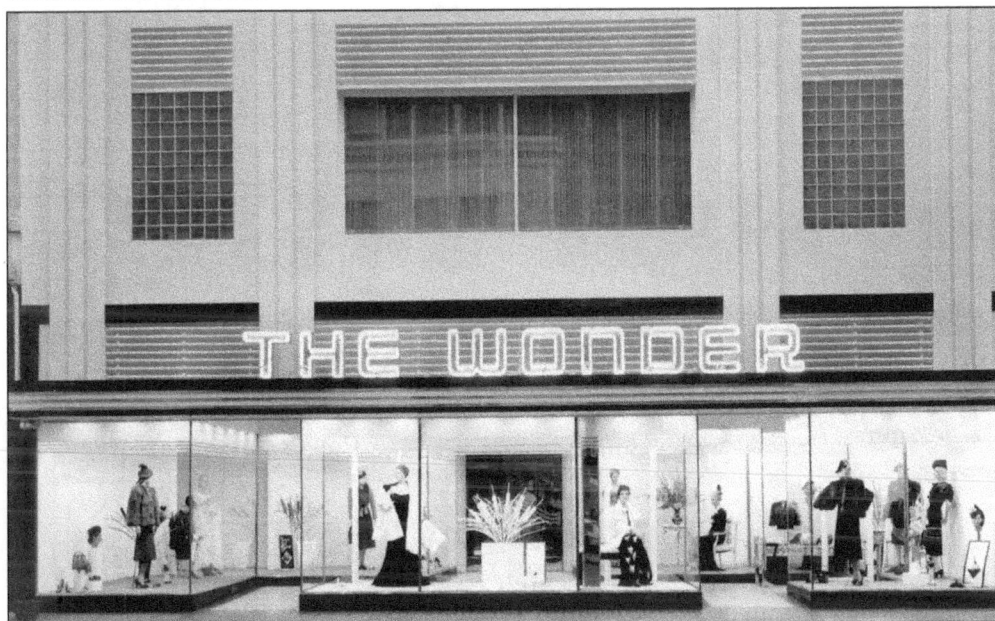

THE WONDER, 1938. The Wonder Ladies Furnishings emanated elegance from the window on Main Street in Stockton. The store was located at 340 Main Street.

HUNTER STREET BETWEEN BRIDGE AND CHANNEL STREETS, C. 1948. The two photographs on this page are of the same building, one was taken before and one after its renovation. This renovation was typical of many that followed the trend toward the Streamline Moderne architectural styles that were sweeping north from Main Street.

HUNTER STREET BETWEEN BRIDGE AND CHANNEL STREETS, C. 1948. This "after" photograph shows a building stripped of its ornamentation to emulate Main Street's adoption of the Moderne influences in architecture. Down the street, the Mansion House was also stripped of ornamentation.

E. ALLEN TEST AUTOMOBILE DEALERSHIP, C. 1931. The impact on American cities following the advent of the automobile was profound, and Stockton was no exception. The E. Allen Test Company began selling Dodge Brothers cars in 1915 at their location on North El Dorado Street. The Test Company was one of Stockton's earliest automobile dealerships.

LLOYD TEST AND CO. NASH DEALERSHIP, C. 1946. In the late 1930s, the Nash automobile company was distinguished by its futuristic thinking and streamlined automobile designs. These qualities appealed to the Stockton market, and the Test Company brought the Streamline Era of modern automobile design to Stockton.

BALLOON ASCENSION, COURTHOUSE PLAZA, JULY 4, 1876. By all accounts of the day, Stocktonians celebrated Independence Day with abandon.

Six

STOCKTON CELEBRATES

Awed by the magnitude of Stockton's agricultural, industrial, and entrepreneurial accomplishments, it is easy to forget that Stockton was once a significant entertainment and recreation destination in California. Its centrally located hotels and transportation systems interconnected a menu of pleasure that once produced Stockton's reputation as a "show town" and sponsor of a must-see county fair. Downtown Stockton offered a unique atmosphere for conventioneers, vacationers, and entertainment seekers. It offered a wholesome, sylvan lifestyle that epitomized the ideal of California living throughout the 20th century. Artesian wells continuously replenished public baths, el fresco dining, and entertainment from rooftops overlooking the city and bountiful farmland. Popular entertainment in theatres and nightclubs made the Stockton experience complete and memorable. Stockton's intimate scale from 1850 to 1930 lent a distinctly homespun quality to its regional and national celebrations that is unlikely to be recreated today in a sprawling modern city approaching a population of a half million.

Stockton was an overtly patriotic city from its beginnings in 1850, and it never missed an opportunity to parade its pride. The popularity of World Expositions and Mechanic's Fairs was at its zenith at the turn of the 20th century. California Admission Day, Independence Day, and Veterans Day were cause for grand parades around the city. The plaza, with the courthouse as backdrop, was the home of annual festivals. Stocktonians built an agricultural hall and pavilion to nourish these events. The legacy of these early institutions is alive in the county fairgrounds and at public festivals and expositions. The county fair was an invention of pioneer optimism and pride, and it perpetuates a legacy, an economy, and a future for Stockton. Even the Potato Day Festival, quirky by today's popular taste and self-image, had a brief life in Stockton and is, in a sense, a forgotten predecessor of today's wildly popular Asparagus Festival.

The future of arts and entertainment in Stockton is widely discussed within the cultural community today, and its history is recorded in Stockton's newspapers. In a city dominated by the industrial arts, the fine arts of dance, painting, and sculpture have generally occupied the nosebleed section of community culture. Several theaters have prospered in Stockton: The Corinthian, the Stockton, the Avon and the Yosemite were the great theaters of the 19th and early 20th centuries, offering live theatre and international celebrities of the day. Live theatre and music were widely available through the 1920s but rapidly succumbed to the cinema and the bright light marquees of the Fox Theatre. The war economy and the gritty, calloused industrialism that spread out of control from the Stockton Channel tarnished the luster of art and entertainment in downtown Stockton for decades into the future. Today, with a new city arts plan in place and a sports complex under construction, there appears to be acknowledgment of the wisdom and assets that arts and recreational venues can contribute to the vitality of urban life, community spirit, commercial prosperity, and the favorable reputation of downtown Stockton.

CENTENNIAL ARCH, JULY 4, 1876. A Centennial Arch was financed, designed, and constructed by J.D. Peters at the intersection of Main and Hunter Streets on the Courthouse Plaza. It read, "E. Pluribus Unum" (We Are One). The I.O.O.F. building is in the background.

MAIN STREET STOCKTON, CENTENNIAL DAY PARADE, JULY 4, 1876. Stockton's centennial parade was one of hundreds of parades that would tread Main Street in the following years.

102

BALLOON ASCENSION, STOCKTON PLAZA, JULY 4, 1876. Capt. P.A. Van Tassel, a popular showman of early Stockton, conducted balloon ascension on the Plaza.

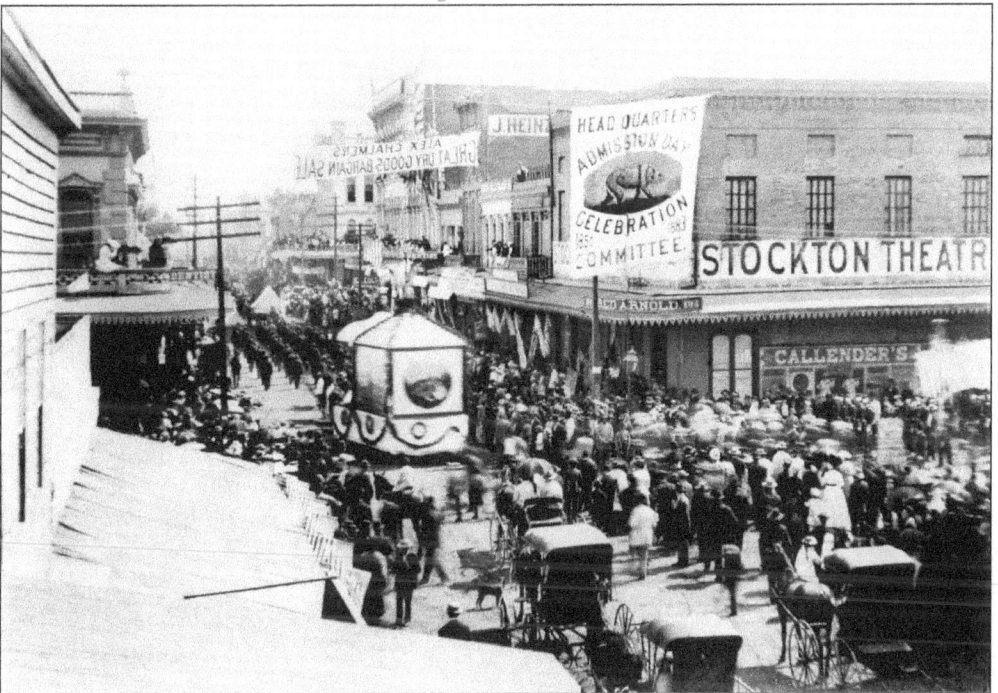

ADMISSION DAY PARADE, SEPTEMBER 9, 1883. The Admission Day parade proceeded east on Main from Commerce Street. The photographer J. Pitcher Spooner took this photograph as the parade passed through the intersection of Main and El Dorado Streets.

THE STOCKTON VOLUNTEER FIRE DEPARTMENT DRESSED FOR PARADE, C. 1865. Opportunities and events to express patriotism were well attended in Stockton's early history. The fire department left the parade early this year to extinguish a fire.

GRAND ARMY OF THE REPUBLIC, NOVEMBER 11, 1919. For an annual celebration and reflection on the "old days," Stockton's Grand Army of the Republic assembled for this photograph in front of the county courthouse.

AMERICAN LEGION PARADE, C. 1942. Parades on Main Street continued well into the late 1940s but experienced a steady decline in the post–World War II period.

POTATO DAY PARADE, C. 1920. The Potato Day parade was short lived as a local and national phenomenon.

AVON THEATRE, C. 1885. The Avon Theatre opened to the public on August 15, 1882, with the play *Hazel Kirke*. The theatre was located on the southeast corner of Main and California Streets. Stage plays were popular in Stockton in the 19th and early 20th centuries. The Avon closed its doors by 1892, upstaged by the elegance of the new Yosemite Theatre.

YOSEMITE THEATRE, C. 1900. The Yosemite Theatre was constructed on the old site of the Agricultural Pavilion (later Methodist Church). It stood as Stockton's premier theatre for nearly 40 years. Lavishly decorated with a capacity for 1,700 guests, it was a significant venue used by entertainers such as Lillie Langtry, John Philip Sousa, and Will Rogers.

NOVELTY THEATRE, c. 1906. The Novelty Theatre opened to the public in 1906. It presented vaudeville, illustrated slides, and Stockton's first motion pictures. It was located on the north side of Weber Avenue between Hunter and San Joaquin Streets.

GOING TO THE FOX, C. 1940. The development of the Fox Theatre in 1930 added luster back to Stockton's reputation for entertainment. Celebrities made regular parades of their arrival en route to the Fox Theatre on Main Street. The theatre reinvigorated Stockton's reputation with an ambitious lineup of popular musical performers such as Duke Ellington, the Dorsey Bothers, and Paul Whiteman.

STOCKTON MUNICIPAL BATHS, C. 1900S. The Stockton Municipal Baths were formerly known as the Jackson Baths. They were located on south San Joaquin Street at Seventh Street, near the present-day McKinley Park. The Weber Baths were also very popular. They were constructed in 1883 on the site of the present-day Hotel Stockton. The water that supplied the baths ran from the courthouse artesian well at 88 degrees.

LINCOLN BEACHY WITH THE CURTIS BIPLANE, STOCKTON FAIRGROUNDS, 1914. Lincoln Beachy was a famous aerial acrobat of his day. He performed in Stockton above Oak Grove Park and the fairgrounds.

M.P. HENDERSON, C. 1880. By the mid-1850s, it was apparent that San Joaquin wheat and agriculture would play an important role in Stockton's economic prosperity and destiny. Agricultural and mechanic fairs were organized annually on the plaza to boost business. M.P. Henderson & Son, one of Stockton's most famous carriage and wagon builders, displayed works under the plaza tents. Henderson wagons became famous as the 20-mule team wagons that hauled borax from the mines of Death Valley.

AGRICULTURE PAVILION, C. 1890. Stockton's Agricultural Pavilion was constructed in 1885 on the block bound by El Dorado, San Joaquin, Washington, and Lafayette. It was a massive wooden structure (38,000 square feet), Stockton's largest auditorium at the time. On September 28, 1902, a legendary fire reduced the structure to embers and caused the death of Fireman Tom Walsh, the first casualty for the Stockton Fire Department.

LOOKING WEST TO THE HEAD OF NAVIGATION FROM THE BALCONY OF THE HOTEL
STOCKTON, 1910. The head of navigation is one of the most significant sites in Stockton's
History. Since the early settlement of city, the head of navigation has been relocated west
on the channel twice from its original designation at Hunter Street (under today's
Hotel Stockton).

LOOKING WEST TO THE HEAD OF NAVIGATION FROM THE BALCONY OF THE HOTEL
STOCKTON, 2004. Today, the head of navigation is located at Center Street. Stockton's
new De Carli Square is visible in the foreground. Five years ago, this site was an elevated
parking lot.

Seven

STANDING AT THE CROSSROADS

One of the many pleasures of making and working with historic photographs of Stockton has been the opportunity to learn something about the history of my city, compare yesterday with today, and envision Stockton's future. I have found the photographic record of Stockton revealing and sobering. It evokes a profound appreciation of the pioneer vision and sheer determination it required for creating and stabilizing this city. The record also poses questions that are fair and reasonable to ask if we wish to participate in a prosperous future for Stockton. Most importantly, it has produced a more informed outlook on the history and future of downtown Stockton, and the challenges currently facing our city leaders and planners. This last chapter presents a brief series of re-photographic views of Stockton from The Stockton Re-photographic Survey, an urban documentary project. They are time-overlays from locations considered to be historically significant in Stockton. They also show evidence of a current urban renaissance underway. Other images return to locations where the city ranges from securely stable to transitional.

My involvement with urban documentary is an integral part of my teaching at the University of the Pacific in Stockton and is one of several opportunities to teach and direct the study of photography within a critical context, a case study of the photographer's role in recording urban history. In the absence of any other systematic effort to document the city, we established the Stockton Re-photographic Survey and an incremental approach to achieving the goal of recording Stockton for future generations. As our archive grows, so too will our legacy to the community. Producing a useful archive for future users requires some strategy. The discipline usually breaks down to making specific types of photographs: broad panoramic views that describe the broader relationships of the city; street intersections where city zoning and the coveted "location" usually produces the most revealing index of stability or change; and more specific typologies of buildings that contain civic, cultural and commercial institutions. It requires accurate data so that others can reliably understand the photographs and possibly return for another look.

Urban documentary photography begins with relatively simple questions that become final with the release of the shutter. We have learned to ask elemental questions about photography. We regularly ask ourselves: "What is important to record?" "When is the right time to record it?" and "What is our field of view?" Contemporary urban documentary photographs rarely inspire audiences addicted to the picturesque. The significance of these photographs accrues and matures with time and Stockton's changing urban space, in the same manner the historical photographs we enjoy today had to undergo. Adding the comparative element of re-photography augments the experience and reaffirms the strength of the medium to mark time. We are no longer as naïve as we once were about the documentary photograph. But we understand that the urban environment is an evolving group of stories. Documentary photographs by themselves are not the stories; they embed layers of artifacts (geographical and autobiographical), they ask questions, and they initiate the quest to know and appreciate Stockton.

THE CORINTHIAN BUILDING, OCTOBER 1851. The Corinthian Building is one of the first hotels in Stockton. It contained the local stagecoach office, restaurant, and theater.

THE DE CARLI PLAZA AND STATE OF CALIFORNIA BUILDING, JULY 2004. The De Carli Plaza is one of Stockton's newest developments. This site is scheduled for additional changes in the near future.

WEBER AVENUE LOOKING EAST FROM MONROE STREET, 1890. Weber Avenue has undergone significant changes since 1850. Through 1945, it served as corridor for industrial traffic and exchange between the wharves and the railroad.

WEBER AVENUE LOOKING EAST FROM MONROE STREET, JULY 2004. Currently, the Weber corridor is in transition. The Sperry Building and the Waterfront Warehouse, two historically significant landmarks, are located along Weber Avenue.

EL DORADO STREET LOOKING NORTH FROM WEBER AVENUE, 1890. El Dorado Street was Stockton's principal north/south corridor. The streets were cobbled in the late 19th century when horse and buggy was the mode of transportation.

EL DORADO STREET LOOKING NORTH FROM WEBER AVENUE, 2004. In the hundred years that elapsed since the image above was made, this site has been completely reconstructed.

114

LOOKING NORTHEAST FROM THE INTERSECTION OF WEBER AVENUE AND HUNTER STREET, c. 1930. In the early 1850s, a slough ran southeast through this intersection and the courthouse was under construction. The Windsor House was constructed in 1873 as the Mansion House.

LOOKING NORTHEAST FROM THE INTERSECTION OF WEBER AVENUE AND HUNTER STREET, AUGUST 2004. While the elemental structures of the 1870s buildings remain, the influence of 1930s Moderne architecture is still present on the Mansion House.

MAIN STREET LOOKING EAST FROM EL DORADO STREET, C. 1890. In the last decades of the 19th century, Main Street was the primary retail entertainment, and public transportation corridor in Stockton.

MAIN STREET LOOKING EAST FROM EL DORADO STREET, JULY 2004. In the 1970s, Main Street was closed and the last of the old city was razed. Today a pedestrian corridor to the Courthouse, Plaza and Main Street has replaced the former street.

MAIN STREET LOOKING EAST FROM HUNTER STREET, 1925. In the early decades of the 20th century, this was the intersection of major crossroads in downtown Stockton. The courthouse is left of center.

MAIN STREET LOOKING EAST FROM HUNTER STREET, JULY 2004. Today, this section of Main Street is part of a small greenbelt and public plaza west of the courthouse.

MAIN STREET LOOKING WEST FROM AMERICAN STREET, C. 1890. This was the last decade of Stockton's early streets and skyline. The new era of the skyscraper on Main Street was just around the corner. Most of the new skyscrapers are still in place today.

MAIN STREET LOOKING WEST FROM AMERICAN STREET, AUGUST 2004. Weekends in the city are quiet and a good time for architectural tours of Main Street and downtown Stockton.

LOOKING NORTHEAST TO SAN JOAQUIN STREET AND MINER AVENUE, 1900. The Methodist Church occupied this corner from 1881 to 1958. The Miner slough also ran through this vicinity, as indicated by the handrail for the bridge on the right side of the photograph.

LOOKING NORTHEAST TO SAN JOAQUIN STREET AND MINER AVENUE, JULY 2004. Today this is a busy intersection for commercial activity.

SUTTER STREET AND MINER AVENUE LOOKING SOUTH, C. 1930. Stockton's business district began to expand north of Main in the 1930s and 1940s. The Medico-Dento Building was the first skyscraper north of Main.

SUTTER STREET AND MINER AVENUE LOOKING SOUTH, JULY 2004. Today this site is a busy intersection for banking, small enterprise, and a significant east-west corridor across the city.

LOOKING SOUTHEAST FROM CALIFORNIA AND MINER AVENUE, 1925. This neighborhood garage was typical of Stockton in the 1920s through the 1940s. It operated near the interface of commercial and residential zones. The commercial signage is a great artifact of its time.

LOOKING SOUTHEAST FROM CALIFORNIA AND MINER AVENUE, AUGUST 2004. Today, while this building and intersection have changed in appearance, an automotive repair shop continues to operate from location.

LOOKING NORTHEAST FROM CALIFORNIA AND MARKET STREET, 1890. In the late 19th century, California Street was the edge of the business district and a northern corridor to the state hospital. Public transportation could be picked up one block north at Main Street.

LOOKING NORTHEAST FROM CALIFORNIA AND MARKET STREET, 2004. Today, this location is on the edge of urban transition. The building on the right is the old Owl Drug Store.

REFERENCES AND SUGGESTED READING

Bonata, Robert E. and Horrace A. Spencer. *Stockton's Historic Public Schools*. Stockton, CA. Stockton Unified School District, 1981.

Cahill, Helen Kennedy. *Captain Weber and His Place in Early California History*. University of the Pacific, Stockton, CA. *Pacific Historian* Vol. 20, No. 4, Winter 1976.

Davis, Olive. *Stockton: Sunrise Port on the San Joaquin*. Woodland Hills, CA. Windsor Publications.

Hammond, George P. *The Weber Era in Stockton History*. Friends of the Bancroft Library. University of California, Berkeley, 1982.

Kennedy, Glenn A. *It Happened in Stockton 1900–1925*. Vol. I–III. Stockton. Self Published.

Martin, V. Covert with R. Coke Wood and Leon Bush. *Stockton Album Through the Years*. Stockton, CA. 1959.

Parsons, James, J. *A Geographer Looks at the San Joaquin Valley*. University of California, Berkeley. James Sauer Memorial. Lecture. 1987.

Spencer, Horrace A. *Railroads of San Joaquin County: An Elementary School Source Book*. Stockton, CA. San Joaquin County Superintendent of Schools, 1976.

Tinkham, George H. *History of San Joaquin County, California, with Biographical Sketches*. Los Angeles, CA: Historic Record Company, 1923.

Wood, Coke R. and Leonard Covello. *Stockton Memories: A Pictorial History of Stockton, California*. Fresno, CA: Valley Publishers, 1977.

Visit us at
arcadiapublishing.com